How to use your Snap Revision Text Guide

This 'DNA' Snap Revision Text Guide will help yc
Literature exam. It is divided into two-page top
the bits you find tricky. This book covers everyth

Plot: what happens in the play?

Setting and Context: what periods, places, ever
understanding the play?

Characters: who are the main characters, how are they presented, and how do
they change?

Themes: what ideas does the author explore in the play, and how are they shown?

The Exam: what kinds of question will come up in your exam, and how can you
get top marks?

To help you get ready for your exam, each two-page topic includes:

Key Quotations to Learn
Short quotations to memorise that will allow you to analyse in the exam and boost
your grade.

Summary
A recap of the most important points covered in the topic.

Sample Analysis
An example of the kind of analysis that the examiner will be looking for.

Quick Test
A quick-fire test to check you can remember the main points from the topic.

Exam Practice
A short writing task so you can practise applying what you've covered in the topic.

Glossary
A handy list of words you will find useful when revising 'DNA' with
easy-to-understand definitions.

 ebook

To access the ebook version of this
Snap Revision Text Guide, visit

collins.co.uk/ebooks
and follow the step-by-step instructions.

AUTHOR:
CHARLOTTE
WOOLEY

Published by Collins
An imprint of HarperCollins*Publishers*
1 London Bridge Street
London SE1 9GF

© HarperCollins*Publishers* Limited 2018

ISBN 9780008306649

First published 2018

10 9 8 7 6 5 4 3 2

British Library Cataloguing in Publication Data.

A CIP record of this book is available from the British Library.

Printed in the United Kingdom.

Commissioning Editor: Gillian Bowman
Managing Editor: Craig Balfour
Author: Charlotte Wooley
Proofreader: Jill Laidlaw
Project manager and editor:
  Project One Publishing Solutions, Scotland
Typesetting: Jouve
Cover designers: Kneath Associates and
  Sarah Duxbury
Production: Natalia Rebow

ACKNOWLEDGEMENTS

DNA © Dennis Kelly, 2008 by kind permission of Oberon Books Ltd

The author and publisher are grateful to the copyright holders for permission to use quoted materials and images.

Every effort has been made to trace copyright holders and obtain their permission for the use of copyright material. The author and publisher will gladly receive information enabling them to rectify any error or omission in subsequent editions. All facts are correct at time of going to press.

MIX
Paper from
responsible source

FSC
www.fsc.org   FSC™ C007454

This book is produced from independently certified FSC™ paper to ensure responsible forest management.

For more information visit:
www.harpercollins.co.uk/green

Contents

Act 1

You must be able to: understand what happens in **Act 1**.

What has happened at the start of the play?

The **exposition** begins by creating an **enigma** between Mark and Jan, which is solved in the second scene where John Tate begins to take control as he has 'looked after things before'.

As entertainment, several teenagers have bullied and tormented an outsider named Adam, making him do silly and dangerous things, like eating 'big fistfuls of leaves' then 'run across a motorway'. Finally, they took him to a shaft covered with a grille, and made him walk over, 'chucking these stones into him'. Adam 'drops' into the hole – they believe he is dead.

They meet in the woods to discuss what to do. John Tate, their leader, is panicking. He tells them 'that word is banned', unable to face the word 'dead'. Their conversation suggests John has arrived relatively recently and become the leader of the group, taking over from Richard.

Surprisingly, Phil takes control, coming up with a plan to make everyone 'think he's been abducted, they'll be inquiries, police, mourning a service and if everyone keeps their mouths shut we should be fine.'

Who leads the group?

At first it seems this is John Tate – he's made the group's lives better and demands they all say they are on 'his side'. There has clearly been conflict in the past with Richard, as they are **antagonistic** towards one another. There is also leadership from Phil, who invents the plan.

What is Phil's plan?

Phil instructs Danny to steal Adam's jumper and give it to Cathy and Mark, who will get a stranger's DNA onto it then leave it to be discovered. He invents a person – 'fat Caucasian male, 5'9' say, with thinning hair'. The precision of his language suggests he's inspired by the media or fictional detective stories. Brian and Richard are to report a flasher in the woods, and the others are to create false footprints. All these clues should lead to the police having a suspect that doesn't exist. Phil and Leah don't have roles in the plan.

What is the symbolism of the bonobos?

In Scene 4, Leah's monologue is a metaphor for human behaviour. She tells Phil there are only small differences between the DNA of chimps, bonobos and humans. She says 'chimps are evil', attacking the weak, whereas 'bonobos are the complete opposite of chimps' and have **empathy** for and take care of the most vulnerable in their society. This **symbolises** the differences in human behaviour. Leah suggests if humans discovered bonobos first we might have a different view of ourselves and therefore behave more kindly to others.

Key Quotations to Learn

JAN: proper dead, not living dead?
MARK: Not living dead, yes. (1.1)

LEAH: I talk too much, so shoot me. So kill me, Phil, call the police, lock me up, rip out my teeth with a pair of rusty pliers. (1.2)

LEAH: I mean they're exactly like chimps, but the tiniest change in their DNA. (1.4)

Summary

- Several of the group believe they have killed Adam.
- They turn to Phil and Leah for help.
- Phil invents a plan to blame an imaginary suspect.

Questions

QUICK TEST
1. What happened to Adam?
2. What is Phil's plan?
3. Who is in charge?
4. What is the symbolism of the bonobos?

EXAM PRACTICE
Using one or more of the 'Key Quotations to Learn', explain how Kelly presents some of his characters in Act 1.

Act 2

You must be able to: understand what happens in Act 2.

What has happened with the police investigation?

The police have identified someone who 'answers the description' Brian and John gave, and 'they've got DNA evidence linking him to the crime'.

When the group meet, it emerges that Cathy and Mark 'showed initiative' and went to the sorting office to find a postman who matched the imaginary description to get his DNA on the jumper, framing an innocent man.

How do relationships within the group change?

Phil becomes more violent, threatening Brian that they will 'swing you onto the grille' and leave him to 'rot' with Adam if he doesn't identify the man framed.

Leah is the voice of logic; she is the only one who repeatedly reminds them 'there wasn't a man in the woods' and the crime was 'non-existent'. She's clearly shocked and upset, not knowing what to do next.

Cathy has become more **callous** and remorseless; the atmosphere at the police station 'was great' and she wants to 'get on the telly' by going back to be interviewed about Adam, as she enjoys the prospect of celebrity.

What is the relevance of Leah's monologues to the plot?

Leah's first **monologue** explores happiness and the natural order – both of which could be assumed to be destroyed by Adam's death. However, Leah's speeches imply that there is no natural order – nobody is happy – and that humanity's chaos is, in fact, the natural way. She wonders if it is 'us that's the anomaly', that humans are the reason for the natural order becoming disturbed. In a shockingly violent line, she reveals to Phil that she has murdered her pet. This could remind an audience of mankind's tendency towards meaningless violence and the theory that no other creature kills through enjoyment or curiosity.

In her second monologue, Leah claims to experience *déjà vu* (the feeling things have happened before) and asks Phil what reality is as 'the world has just changed', suggesting that she is having trouble dealing with what they have done. She wonders if people are 'doomed to behave like people before us', which implies that there is a sense of inevitability (and lack of responsibility) to their actions.

Key Quotations to Learn

LEAH: I took him out of his cage, I put the point of a screwdriver on his head and I hit it with a hammer. (2.2)

LEAH: I mean I'm not being fussy or anything, but the man who kidnapped Adam doesn't actually exist, does he. Well does he?
LOU: No. But they've got him. (2.3)

CATHY: I thought, you know, show initiative, we'll look for a fat balding postman with bad teeth. (2.3)

Summary

- The police have found someone fitting the description, and with the right DNA evidence.
- Cathy and Mark put the DNA of someone matching the description Brian gave on the jumper.
- Brian doesn't want to go back to the police, but Phil threatens to kill him if he doesn't.
- Leah says that most people are happier since Adam's death, apart from John Tate.

Questions

QUICK TEST
1. What has happened in the investigation?
2. How do the police have DNA evidence for the suspect?
3. Why does Leah talk about happiness and the natural order?
4. How does Leah react to the investigation's progress?
5. What happens between Phil and Brian?

EXAM PRACTICE
Using one or more of the 'Key Quotations to Learn', explain how Kelly develops his characters in Act 2.

Act 3

You must be able to: understand the way that the situation changes in Act 3.

Why does Leah threaten to run away?

In Leah's first monologue, she tells Phil she's 'out of here, I'm gone ... I'm running away'. He ignores her dramatic statement and 'says nothing'. Although she says she wants to discover the world, it's clear to the audience the situation is overwhelming her as she immediately begins talking about the memorial service. Her comments **foreshadow** her leaving at the end of Act 3. She uses **meta-theatrical** language ('exit stage left Leah'), which draws attention to the constructed nature of the play.

As her dialogue continues she says that the murder has made the group better people – they are behaving well towards others, and grief has made 'everyone feel wonderful' because they have something to bond over. John Tate and Brian are the exceptions; John hasn't been 'seen in weeks' and Brian is 'off his head' and on medication.

How have other people reacted to Adam's death?

From what Leah tells Phil, Adam's death **precipitates** a wave of generosity and self-reflection. She describes everyone as happy, as though the reality of Adam's death has made them value their own lives more.

Cathy is exploiting the situation to become 'like a celebrity, there are second years asking for her autograph', while Brian and John Tate have found their lives falling apart.

What happens to Adam?

Cathy finds him in 'living in a hedge' and brings him to the group. He tells them he has been living there since finding his way out of the grille and eating whatever he could find.

What is Phil's solution?

He threateningly instructs Cathy to take Adam and Brian to the hedge and tells her 'he can't come back' – implying that she should murder Adam for real this time. He places a plastic bag on Brian's head until he struggles to breathe, **implicitly** showing Cathy what she should do with Adam. This does happen offstage, which could suggest that Brian is also physically involved. However, the changes in the group and its leadership suggest it is Cathy who does it.

How does Leah and Phil's relationship change?

Leah protests when Phil tells Cathy to take Adam back. She says they can 'explain, we can talk ... and make them understand' but Phil ignores her.

In the field she doesn't speak – there are no more monologues from her – even when Phil offers her a Starburst. She takes a sweet but then spits it out, bursts into tears, 'storms off' and leaves him.

Key Quotations to Learn

LEAH: I felt terrible of course, but everyone felt wonderful. It's incredible. The change. This place. You're a miracle worker. Everyone's happy. (3.2)

[Adam] stands there twitchily, staring at them as though they were aliens and it looks as though he might run off at any moment. (3.3)

ADAM: I felt like the dark was my fear, do you know what I mean? I was wrapped in it. Like a soft blanket. (3.3)

Summary

- Leah tells Phil she wants to run away.
- Leah says since Adam died, people seem happier or are using the situation to their advantage, like Cathy.
- Cathy finds Adam living in a hedge.
- Phil instructs Cathy to take Brian and Adam to the hedge and kill Adam.
- Leah stops talking to Phil, cries and leaves.

Questions

QUICK TEST
1. What does Leah want to do at the start of Act 3?
2. What does Leah say about how people's lives have changed since Adam's death?
3. What really happened to Adam?
4. What does Phil do to Brian?
5. How does Phil and Leah's relationship change?

EXAM PRACTICE
Using one or more of the 'Key Quotations to Learn', write a paragraph explaining how Kelly creates a tense atmosphere in Act 3.

Act 4

You must be able to: understand the way that Dennis Kelly creates a resolution in Act 4.

What has happened to the main characters by the end of the play?

Several characters' lives are destroyed by what has happened. Brian is having a breakdown as 'they're going to **section** him.'

Danny is doing work experience at a dentist's but hates it and 'can't stand the cavities ... it feels like you're going to fall in', an allusion to the grille into which Adam fell, showing his inability to come to terms with what happened.

John Tate has 'found god', trying to convert people to make amends for his part in the death.

Cathy has taken over running things, with Lou supporting her, and has become more violent and unpredictable, with rumours that she 'cut a first year's finger off'.

Jan and Mark have started shoplifting and building a network of supply and demand.

What has happened to Leah?

Jan and Mark's opening **duologue** indicates that Leah has moved schools, which reminds the audience how young they are. They don't actually name her but wonder if Phil knows.

She didn't tell anybody that she was leaving, and nobody knows where she has gone.

How is Act 4's structure different from Acts 1–3?

Act 4 has only two scenes whereas the previous three acts each have four scenes.

The group scene has disappeared, indicating that they are all separated from one another, further reflected in the final scene.

The final scene takes place in the field, but with Richard and Phil rather than Leah and Phil. Phil doesn't respond to Richard despite his desperate bids for attention like walking on his hands. Phil 'is not eating', symbolising his lost appetite for life after losing Leah – he is even less enthusiastic than he was.

Key Quotations to Learn

Phil is not eating. He stares into the distance. Silence. (4.2)

RICHARD: Can't stand the cavities, he says when they open their mouths sometimes it feels like you're going to fall in. (4.2)

RICHARD: She's insane. She cut a first year's finger off, that's what they say anyway. (4.2)

RICHARD: [For] a second, as I was coming up here I felt like I was an alien in a cloud. (4.2)

Summary

- Brian and Danny's lives have been ruined, while John Tate has turned to religion.
- Cathy and Lou are running things, while Mark and Jan shoplift.
- Leah has moved schools without telling anyone.
- Phil stops eating in response to Leah's disappearance, and to what has happened.
- Act 4 only has two scenes, reflecting the fragmented state of the group.

Sample Analysis

Kelly ends the play with a lost empty feeling as only Richard and Phil are onstage and *'they sit in silence.'* By removing Leah from the final act (which has a different **structure** as a result), Kelly demonstrates the destabilisation that has occurred in the characters' worlds. The *'silence'* at the end should be timed to give the audience a moment of reflection to consider their responses to the events and individuals in the play, whether they feel any empathy for them or condemn them entirely.

Questions

QUICK TEST
1. How have the characters' lives changed?
2. How is Act 4 structurally different?
3. What does the missing group scene represent?
4. Who joins Phil in the field?

EXAM PRACTICE
Using one or more of the 'Key Quotations to Learn', write a paragraph analysing the ways that Kelly presents characters at the end of the play.

Narrative Structure

You must be able to: analyse the significance of the way Kelly has structured the play.

What is the timescale of the play?

The action takes place over a few weeks, with gaps between each act in which the police investigation continues, and the **dynamics** of the characters change.

How is the play structured?

There are four acts, performed in approximately 90 minutes (1.5 hours), without an interval. This is a relatively short time-frame and creates a fast-**paced** series of actions. This **echoes** the way the actions in the play feel to the characters, particularly Leah, as though they are spiralling out of control and cannot be stopped.

Where does the play take place?

The first three acts cycle through the same four **settings**:

- Jan and Mark in a street
- Leah and Phil in a field
- The group in a wood
- Leah and Phil in a field.

This repetitive structure suggests events occur **cyclically,** without possibility of change. This connects with Leah's comment that people are 'doomed to behave like people before us'. This quote and the structure of scenes suggest there is no way out for the group; they are trapped in their situation.

How does the final act change?

The final act has only two scenes: Jan and Mark in a street, then Richard and Phil in a field. By removing the group scenes, Kelly presents the fractured state of the group; their lack of cohesion questions how solid their bonds were originally. Kelly could be suggesting that things can change – they can escape the 'trap' of the first three acts – but that they aren't necessarily moving to a better situation.

What is the significance of the ending?

Leah's relationship with Phil has broken down. She is replaced by Richard, but Phil is 'silent' and 'not eating', which suggests that he is affected by her departure. He might also be struggling to come to terms with the events of the play, but this would be surprising as he has previously appeared to be a cold character.

Richard's speech sounds much like Leah's, indicating that people are perhaps much the same as one another, making the audience question whether they would behave the same way in these situations.

The final **stage directions** instruct silence – Kelly suggests language has become useless and cannot undo the damage done.

Key Quotations to Learn

LEAH: We're in trouble now, Phil. Don't know how this'll pan out. Trouble now. (1.4)

MARK: He's not going.
JAN: What do you mean he's not going? (2.1)

No answer. They sit in silence. End. (4.2)

Summary

- The action takes place over a few weeks.
- The play is four acts, without an interval, creating a quick pace as the events spiral out of control.
- The repetitive nature of the scenes suggests that human nature is inescapable and unchangeable.
- The ending symbolises the breakdown in the characters' relationships and their failure to communicate further.

Sample Analysis

Mark and Jan's duologues open each act *in media res*, creating an impression that action is occurring **offstage** and time has moved forward. At the opening of Act 3, Mark says 'Cathy found him in the woods', creating an enigma just as in Act 1 when they say 'he's dead.' These short utterances cause the audience to question who they are referring to and what has happened. Moving the action forward in this way creates a quicker pace, and makes it feel as though the events the characters describe are moving too fast for them to control.

Questions

QUICK TEST
1. What is the effect of the timing of the play?
2. What is the effect of the cyclical structure of each act?
3. How does the final act change?
4. What is the significance of Phil and Richard's relationship at the end?

EXAM PRACTICE
Write a paragraph exploring how Kelly uses the repetitive structure of his play to explore the nature of isolation.

Perceptions of 21st Century Youth

You must be able to: understand the way that Kelly is influenced by modern perceptions of young people.

How does Kelly explore ideas about young people?

The play's characters are disaffected and alienated. John Tate describes them being a small group, a clique or gang, separated from others: 'Aren't things better? For us? I mean, not for them out there, but for us?'

The **social institutions** that are mentioned – police, school – are generic and have little impact on the teenage characters. The only ways they involve adults in the situation are to influence their interpretation of events. For example, Richard is told to 'take Brian to the Head' to tell him about the flasher, and they plant DNA evidence for the police.

This makes the play relevant to wider society as the more generic the institutions are, the more audiences can see them reflected in their own social experience. It also suggests the alienation of the characters, as they don't see these institutions as supportive or protective, but as something to be used and guarded against. Leah is the only character to suggest involving them, but her language is vague. She says 'we can go through the whole thing and make them understand', which suggests there is a **binary opposition** between the characters ('we') who are one unit, and 'them', which represents adults and society in general.

What are some of the perceptions of young people that Kelly explores?

Around the time Kelly was writing (2007) there was a **moral panic** about young people. ASBOs (anti-social behaviour orders) were introduced and popularly thought to target young people. The **dehumanising** of young people, calling them 'hoodies' rather than acknowledging their humanity and, often, their valid social problems, refused to see society's responsibility for their behaviour.

Tabloid newspapers (often dominated by sensationalism) furthered this image with headlines blaming young people for a moral decline and associating them with excessive drinking, sex and violence. A study at the time Kelly was writing showed that half of tabloid stories about teenage boys were about crime, using language like 'yob', 'lout', and 'thug'. Around 85% of teenage boys thought that newspapers portrayed them negatively. Kelly uses these perceptions to suggest that the way they behave might be a reaction to society's lack of trust – if society doesn't trust them, then they can't trust it to look after them either.

How does Kelly use modern technology?

Although the play is written in 2007, it doesn't use technology (e.g. mobile phones, social media) that would affect most teens' lives. Instead, the characters meet face to face. This is a dramatic choice, as having characters onstage together is a very different experience for an audience.

Cathy's obsession with television celebrity could reflect modern interest in celebrity, particularly the increase in YouTube, Instagram and reality TV stars, and many teenagers' desire to be famous.

Key Quotations to Learn

JOHN TATE: Lou, are you scared of anyone in this school?
LOU: You? (1.3)

DANNY: You need three references for dental college, how am I gonna get references? (2.3)

LEAH: Cathy was on the telly. Used that clip on every channel. She's like a celebrity. (3.2)

Summary

- The characters are alienated from society. Social institutions have little impact on their lives.
- There is an opposition between the characters and the rest of society, maintained by their feelings of isolation.
- In the late 2000s there was a moral panic about young people's changing behaviour and moral decline.
- Kelly's choice not to include mobile phones is a dramatic one.

Questions

QUICK TEST
1. How do the characters interact with social institutions?
2. What impressions of young people did tabloid newspapers of the day present?
3. Why doesn't Kelly use mobile phones?
4. How does Cathy relate to modern celebrity?

EXAM PRACTICE
Relating your ideas to the social contexts, write a paragraph analysing the ways that Kelly presents modern youth through one of his characters.

Theatrical Devices

You must be able to: understand the way that Kelly uses theatrical devices to present his ideas.

How does Kelly approach setting?

The generic settings – 'a field, a street and a wood' – are vague, enabling directors to place the play in their own communities. This makes it relatable, implying that the teenagers could be found anywhere – anyone is susceptible to this kind of situation.

What impact does gender have?

Kelly's opening note says 'Names and genders of characters are suggestions only and can be changed to suit performers'. This arbitrary assignment of gender questions ideas of 'masculine' and 'feminine'. For example, the original casting could **subvert** stereotypes of leadership. John and Phil are leaders at first, but Cathy takes over their roles using violence, which could be an unusual association with femininity. However, if roles are reversed and Cathy is cast as male then her eventual leadership – taking over from a female-cast John and Phil – could be a suggestion that men (Cathy) dominate through violence.

How does Kelly use silence onstage?

Kelly depicts silence and hesitations through stage directions including *Beat. Pause.* These both create moments of silence. A **pause** is a longer moment. Contrastingly, beats are quicker and signify a quick shift in a character or relationship. When John Tate says, '"I'm going to hurt you, actually." *Beat*', the 'beat' is a moment of disbelief from Richard before he replies 'You?'

What is in-yer-face theatre?

In-yer-face theatre is a genre presenting shocking or controversial material. It is **visceral**, forcing audiences to react. It challenges conventional distinctions that define us, such as good/bad, right/wrong – for example, considering the decisions made when covering up Adam's 'death'.

Kelly's work has elements of this style's shocking actions. His characters are blunt, speaking modern **slang**, for example, when Mark describes making Adam 'nick some vodka' and calls him a 'complete nutter'.

How does Kelly use theatrical techniques?

Kelly uses minimal set, costume and props – mainly related to Phil's food, for example, his '*ice cream*' and the '*paper plate ... [he] places a waffle on it*'. This keeps the production **representational** rather than **naturalistic**. Audiences are encouraged to suspend disbelief, and remember the constructed nature of the play, so that they think about the themes and ideas Kelly is exploring.

Leah's monologue (3.2) briefly breaks the **fourth wall** when speaking to Phil:

'It's a big world, Phil, it's a lot bigger than you and me, a lot bigger than all this, these people, sitting here ... don't try and stop me, because, because exit stage left Leah, right now.'

Her phrase 'these people' indicates the audience and could be jarring but reminds them of the play's deliberate construction. Using meta-theatrical language ('stage left') also brings the building of the theatre back into the audience's consciousness and prevents them seeing the events as **cathartic**. Kelly intends the audience to be unsettled at the end and to reflect on the questions raised, such as the moral responsibilities of the characters and what the 'right thing' to do was after Adam's first death, and how far through the play the characters were sympathetic, despite them being killers.

Key Quotations to Learn

Takes place in a street, a field and a wood. (Introduction)

Names and genders of characters are suggestions only. (Introduction)

LEAH: It's a lot bigger than you and me, a lot bigger than all this, these people, sitting here. (3.2)

Summary

- Kelly's settings are generic, which enables directors to interpret them freely.
- Characters' genders are not fixed, raising questions over what is 'masculine' or 'feminine.'
- Beats or pauses suggest silence, with different effects.
- In-yer-face theatre is shocking or controversial, to challenge audience's ideas.
- Kelly's techniques draw attention to the construction of theatre to make the audience think about the issues being explored.

Questions

QUICK TEST
1. What effect do the generic settings have?
2. What impact does the assignment of gender have?
3. What is the difference between a beat and a pause?
4. Why can the play be called 'in-yer-face' theatre?
5. How does Kelly draw attention to the constructed nature of theatre?

EXAM PRACTICE
Relating your ideas to the social contexts, write a paragraph analysing the way Kelly has used one of these theatrical devices to present his themes.

Settings and the Title

You must be able to: explain the symbolic way that Kelly has used settings and the title to present his ideas.

What are the settings used?

Kelly has three settings that rotate – 'a field, a street and a wood'.

What is the symbolism of the settings?

The settings' **atmosphere** represents the connection (or lack of) between the characters and their society. Kelly explores spaces where teenagers congregate, but where they aren't under adult authority.

The town is modern, representing everyday Britain, with the 'sorting office' where Mark and Cathy get DNA, and Mark's explanation 'by the Asda' when Phil describes planting evidence. These generic settings could be anywhere as Kelly wants the audience to feel that the events could happen where they live.

How do the settings represent the characters' relationships?

The public nature of the settings changes cyclically. Scenes transition from 'the street', open and overlooked, where Mark and Jan's cryptic duologues create enigmas. The settings then become more private and hidden (the field, the wood).

Group conversations happen in the most secretive place, the wood, which is symbolic of privacy but is also a space outside society. The group meet here before Adam's death – John Tate asks, 'doesn't everyone want to be us, come here in the woods?' – because they feel like outsiders, searching for somewhere outside the confines of normal society. The wood also represents a space where teenagers gather precisely because it is hidden from adults.

The field is potentially romantic because it is open, rural and secluded. However, although Leah might see it this way, Phil doesn't.

What is the symbolism of the title?

In her monologue on bonobos and chimpanzees, Leah says 'the tiniest change in their DNA' causes bonobos to be empathetic and welcoming to strangers in comparison to the chimpanzees, who cast the weak out of their packs. Kelly uses this as a metaphor for the teenagers' reactions, implying that they behave like chimps but should be more caring like bonobos.

DNA is used in Phil's plan to cover up Adam's death: 'The man picks it up, runs after you covering it in DNA and then gives it back'. This perhaps demonstrates some influence from television drama, where DNA evidence is found at crime scenes. It also implies that DNA evidence is unquestionable proof of crime. This, however, is disproved when Cathy and Mark obtain DNA from someone who fits the description Phil has invented. It also makes the web of deceit impossible to untangle, because they would have to explain how the DNA came to be on Adam's jumper.

Summary

- Kelly uses three settings, to represent characters and their isolation.
- The town could be anywhere, suggesting the events could happen everywhere.
- The scenes move from an open setting to increasingly private settings.
- The wood is the most secretive place, representing the characters' isolation from society.

Sample Analysis

Kelly uses settings to suggest the alienation and loneliness of the characters. Through the repetition of 'a street, a field and a wood', Kelly uses spaces that are isolated and outside the normal social spaces. Even the 'street' is private, as there is nobody else around to overhear the conversations. The characters might seek out community, which is demonstrated as the **ensemble** always meet in the wood together, but they aren't able to connect with the rest of society. This also explores being a teenager as a time when teens often seek out places that are separated from society, so they can learn their own social rules and understandings.

Questions

QUICK TEST
1. What are the three settings?
2. What is the symbolism of each location?
3. How do the private/public nature of the spaces reflect the characters' relationships?
4. What is the symbolism of the title?

EXAM PRACTICE
Relating your ideas to the social contexts, write a paragraph exploring how Kelly uses settings to present one of his themes.

Mark and Jan

You must be able to: analyse the way that Mark and Jan are presented, and their importance in the play.

How do Mark and Jan guide an audience?

Mark and Jan act as a **chorus** or **narrator**. They are often the pair who describe the events that have happened offstage, including Adam's death. This was a feature of Greek tragedy, which often used a chorus to comment on the action.

Their duologues at the beginning of the acts create enigmas, for example, in Act 1 ('Dead?' 'Yeah') and Act 2 ('He's not going.' 'What do you mean he's not going?'). These propel the group – and the audience – into the next phase of the plot.

How responsible are Mark and Jan?

They were both bullies who 'killed' Adam. Jan attempts to defend herself, as she left early, but Mark says it was only because she had to be home 'otherwise, you did all the ...' implying they are all responsible. He even blames Adam, arguing 'you know what he's like' as though Adam's eagerness to be a part of the group makes him a deserving **victim**. The phrase 'you know' creates a relationship with the rest of the group, ganging up on Adam.

Elsewhere, Mark is slow to accept responsibility for framing an innocent man. When Richard greets him 'you dick, Mark,' Mark immediately knows what he is referring to and quickly blames Cathy: 'It was her idea!' The defensive exclamation shows he is unwilling to accept that he could have stopped the process, although others blame him.

They seem younger than the others, looking to the rest of the group for answers. They use slang ('pegging', 'nutter'), which emphasises their age but also serves to contrast the seriousness of what they are describing.

What is the effect of Mark and Jan's language?

Mark and Jan use short **utterances**, often only a word or two long, with frequent interruptions over one another. They repeat one another's dialogue regularly, and this is often to persuade themselves that they are justified:

> MARK: having a laugh really, he was laughing.
> JAN: and crying, soles of his feet.
> MARK: or crying, sort of, a bit of both.

This back-and-forth is **stichomythia**, commonly used by the chorus in Greek drama; it highlights their role as narrators and guides for the audience.

Key Quotations to Learn

MARK: We were having a laugh, weren't we … (1.3)

JAN: Let us punch him.
MARK: he was laughing
JAN: In the face.
MARK: He was laughing.
JAN: at first. (1.3)

JAN: Are we going to be in trouble.
PHIL: If you go now and say nothing to no one about this, you won't be in trouble. (3.3)

Summary

- Mark and Jan are a chorus, or narrators.
- They describe what happens offstage and create an enigma for the audience.
- They repeat each other's phrases, to reassure or justify themselves.
- They don't accept responsibility for their actions, blaming the group.
- Mark, with Cathy, gets the postman's DNA on Adam's jumper.

Sample Analysis

Kelly uses Mark and Jan as a chorus to create enigmas for the audience as well as comedy. Their duologue can be comedic ('JAN: proper dead, not living dead? / MARK: Not living dead, yes'), through the combination of quick-fire responses and the repetition of lines like 'living dead.' However, the comedy is dark – this is an enigma at the opening of the play which becomes solved, temporarily, in the next scene when Adam's death is revealed and the audience might feel guilty for laughing at a serious situation. It also foreshadows Adam's return when he does become 'living dead' to the group.

Questions

QUICK TEST
1. How do Mark and Jan act as narrators?
2. How responsible are Mark and Jan?
3. What is the effect of their language?

EXAM PRACTICE
Using one of the 'Key Quotations to Learn', write a paragraph analysing the ways that Kelly presents Mark and Jan.

You must be able to: analyse the way that Phil is presented, and his importance in the play.

How is Phil presented?

He is calculating: he plans the cover-up with clear instructions – 'do not use the first one on the roll, use the third or fourth' – which show his intelligence and his coldness.

He plans Adam's death, justifying it to Leah by saying Adam is 'happy' in the woods and 'doesn't want to come back'. Arguing 'what difference will it make?' presents him as callous, prioritising the group's lives over the life of an individual.

How does Phil control other characters?

Phil has previously been on the fringes of the group rather than leading it – he's not involved in the murder. This fits with his uninterested attitude, as he seems to see the group as an interruption, for example, when he's eating his waffle.

Phil doesn't carry out actions but instructs others, positioning him as a leader. Though he claims to have their best interests at heart he will sacrifice an individual (Adam) for the good of the group. He uses violence and threats, telling Brian 'we'll swing you onto the grille'. He gives implicit instructions such as 'he can't come back, Cathy', distancing himself from her actions.

His closest relationship is with Leah. He controls her by withdrawing attention, forcing her to do bizarre and dangerous things to get it back, like threatening to strangle herself.

How does Phil change?

Phil is usually eating. He doesn't speak much but observes those nearby. Eating means he can watch without being observed. His eating creates **black comedy**, like when he decides his waffle *'needs more jam'* and then *'The waffle is ready. Phil looks pleased'* and is immediately interrupted by Mark and Jan.

He ignores Leah too, by offering minimal responses. In their final scene he shows physical affection, as he 'puts his arm around her'. This could seem affectionate and loving but is surprising as he hasn't done this before. It could also demonstrate his complete control of her as she has agreed to follow him in orchestrating Adam's death. This action could, however, be coercive, as it comes at a moment when Leah is vulnerable. His change in attitude causes her to 'stare' and 'storm off', perhaps as she realises his manipulation. In the final scene, he is 'not eating', symbolising the breakdown of their relationship.

Key Quotations to Learn

PHIL: We'll throw rocks at you until you drop through. You'll drop through. You'll fall into the cold. Into the dark. You'll land on Adam's corpse and you'll rot together. (2.3)

PHIL: I'm in charge. Everyone is happier. What's more important; one person or everyone? (3.3)

Phil goes to [Lou]. Places a hand on her shoulder, smiles, warm, reassuring. (3.3)

Summary

- Phil is constantly eating, which gives him opportunities to listen to others.
- His relationship with Leah is controlling and breaks down after Adam's real death.
- Phil plans the cover-up of Adam's death, and then plans to really kill him when he reappears.
- Phil is cold towards individuals, using violence and intimidation to persuade them to do things his way.

Sample Analysis

Kelly presents Phil as a cold, calculating character. When he plans the cover-up he says 'they'll be inquiries, police, mourning a service and ... we should be fine. Any questions?' The final phrase is **rhetorical**; they are clearly shocked by his clear-thinking response and the quick, calculating way he comes up with an effective plan to get away with murder. The list of events makes the process sound straightforward and easy to accomplish, reassuring the group as though nothing significant has happened.

Questions

QUICK TEST
1. What role does Phil play in the group?
2. How does Phil control others?
3. How does his relationship with Leah change?
4. What is the purpose of Phil's eating?

EXAM PRACTICE
Using one of the 'Key Quotations to Learn', write a paragraph analysing how Phil is presented as a character who is in control.

You must be able to: analyse the way that Leah is presented, and her importance in the play.

What do Leah's monologues represent?

In most of Leah's scenes with Phil she has a virtual monologue while he sits almost silently. She explores big ideas – 'who says we're all supposed to be happy,' the 'brutal terror' of life, that 'reality is not what we think'. Her speeches are meandering and lack focus, but she is the one **philosophising**, addressing the big questions of life.

The long monologues also create an expectation of Leah as **garrulous**. Her silence with Phil in Act 3 Scene 4 tells the audience how much has changed, because she is refusing to speak.

How does Leah dramatise situations?

In scenes with Phil, she threatens to hurt herself, grabbing her own throat, argues in **fragmented sentences** as though anticipating his side of an argument, and threatens to leave.

She is also unexpectedly violent at times, for example, showing Phil the hamster she has killed when she 'hit it with a hammer'. She also strangles herself in an attempt to make Phil pay attention to her, demonstrating the lengths she is willing to go to in order to win some affection.

How does Leah relate to other characters?

She is logical, reasoning with others, especially when the postman is arrested: 'they need fibres, they need samples, they need evidence'.

She is **naive** in Act 3. When Adam reappears, she realises they have a responsibility to come forward to the authorities. She argues 'we can explain, we can talk. We can go through the whole thing'. She thinks Phil plans to leave him in the woods and worries about him coming back 'next week, next year', rather than understanding that Phil intends to kill Adam.

What is the significance of her relationship with Phil?

She constantly wants his attention, frequently repeating his name and demanding that he respond to her. However, she physically rejects him at the end as she 'spits the sweet out' and 'storms off'. This is immediately after Phil 'puts his arm around her', which could suggest she sees this as a calculating, even coercive, move. As he hasn't previously shown her any physical affection it seems that this could be a final way to exert his control. Although earlier she wants affection at almost any cost, now the cost is too high for her to bear.

Key Quotations to Learn

LEAH: You can see the incredibly precious beauty and fragility of reality and it's the same for happiness. (2.2)

LEAH: Because there is now a man in prison linked to a non-existent crime ... (2.3)

LEAH: Do you think people always feel like that? D'you think we're doomed to behave like people before us did? (2.4)

Suddenly she stops chewing and spits the sweet out. Gets up, stares at Phil. Storms off. (3.4)

Summary

- Leah's monologues engage with philosophical questions connected with the themes of the play.
- She is dramatic, threatening to leave or harm herself.
- She is logical and reasonable with others.
- She is naive, not realising Phil intends to kill Adam.
- Her silence at the end demonstrates the depth of her despair.

Sample Analysis

Kelly presents Leah's insecurities through her monologues, which are often fragmented: 'I talk too much, what a crime, what a sin, what an absolute catastrophe ... you're not perfect, actually, Phil'. Her list seems an overreaction to his silence, suggesting she is trying but failing to make contact with him. Her use of 'actually' makes her sound more defensive and angry, looking at his failings to avoid facing her own. The meandering nature of her monologues realistically presents her thought process, jumping from one idea to another to attempt to make a connection with Phil.

Questions

QUICK TEST
1. How does Leah behave with Phil?
2. What is the significance of her monologues?
3. What does she want to do with Adam?

EXAM PRACTICE
Using one of the 'Key Quotations to Learn', write a paragraph analysing the ways that Kelly presents the character of Leah.

You must be able to: analyse the way that the character of Cathy is presented, and her importance in the play.

How is Cathy presented at the beginning of the play?

Initially Cathy seems to be a minor character; she stirs up trouble with short utterances ('You shut up', 'He's on Richard's side') designed to **aggravate** the others.

She characterises Adam's death as exciting, a good thing because it makes their lives more dramatic. When she goes to the police station she relishes the limelight and goes back to be interviewed on television – 'They might even give me money for it, do you think I should ask for money?' – enjoying new status as a local celebrity associated with Adam.

What is Cathy's role in the cover-up?

She and Mark must get DNA evidence on to Adam's jumper, tricking a man into touching it.

It is Cathy's idea to go to the sorting office and find someone matching the fake description ('We showed initiative'). This reflects her enjoyment of the **melodrama** of the situation and her love of stirring up trouble without caring about the consequences.

Where does Cathy's power come from?

Cathy is willing to do things others won't, including Phil – she is the one to commit deliberate murder. She gains power in Act 1 by causing trouble, and this develops into taking control over people's lives and deaths by the end.

If Cathy is played female as originally cast, her violence and assumption of leadership at the end could be taken as challenging traditional female characteristics. In contrast, Lou and Leah both follow instructions or respond passively – even Leah's departure isn't an open challenge to male authority. However, Cathy learns from the male characters, particularly Phil, until she is in charge of the group.

How does Cathy change through the play?

Cathy becomes increasingly violent. She slaps Brian and threatens Adam to make him leave the hedge. When Phil shows her how to kill Brian, putting a plastic bag over his head, she leads Adam away intending to 'play a game', a **euphemism** for killing him.

By the end she has become the leader, enjoying the violence and the control it gives her. There are rumours about the violence she has done to others. She delights in the power she has over others.

Key Quotations to Learn

CATHY: I mean, it's quite exciting as well, though, isn't it [...] Better than ordinary life. (1.3)

CATHY: I'm gonna go back [...] get on the telly. (2.3)

PHIL: You and Cathy are going to play a game. With Adam. (3.3)

Summary

- Cathy enjoys causing conflict and upsetting others.
- She enjoys the dramatic element of Adam's death and the celebrity it brings her.
- She plants DNA evidence on Adam's jumper, deliberately seeking someone who fits the made-up description.
- Cathy becomes increasingly violent, eventually leading Brian offstage to kill Adam.

Sample Analysis

Kelly presents Cathy as increasingly violent. When she finds Adam, she 'threatened to gouge one of his eyes out' to force him to come with her. The **verb** 'gouge' is visceral and grotesque, a gory image that demonstrates her character development: she is no longer simply excited by drama but actively creates it. Her language uses **clichés**, but Cathy uses phrases inspired by the media to create her own dramatic scene, fuelling her excitement. These self-representations play into tabloid perceptions of teenagers as self-centred and violent in a glamorised way.

Questions

QUICK TEST
1. What is Cathy like at the beginning of the play?
2. How has she changed by the end?
3. What is her role in the cover-up?
4. What is her response to Adam's death?
5. When is she seen to enjoy power?

EXAM PRACTICE
Using one of the 'Key Quotations to Learn', write a paragraph analysing the ways that Kelly presents the changes in Cathy's character.

You must be able to: analyse the way that the character of Brian is presented, and his importance in the play.

How is Brian presented at the beginning of the play?

The first time the audience sees Brian he is with Cathy, 'crying' over their situation. Throughout, he is one of the weakest characters. Brian says, 'I think we should tell someone' – his first response is to go to adults for help. This makes him seem more childish than the other characters, who want to look after themselves.

In Phil's plan, Brian is the one to go to the Head claiming to have been flashed in the woods. This suggests the others see him as weak, choosing him to pretend to be a victim.

How does Brian change through the play?

Brian cries again the second time he is onstage because he needs to identify the man in police custody as the flasher, but he is unable to lie to the police. When Adam returns, Brian has reverted to a childish, almost infantile manner – he sings, speaks repetitively and expresses all his inner thoughts ('I wonder what earth tastes like') – as though trying to escape reality by becoming a child again. By the end, Brian has suffered a nervous breakdown and may be sectioned. Richard tells Phil that he is on 'stronger and stronger medication ... staring at a wall and drooling'.

Other than Adam, Brian is perhaps the most affected by the situation, as he can't escape the guilt of what they have done.

How could Brian be interpreted as a victim?

Like Adam, Brian is a victim of the others' bullying. He is weak, unable to hide his emotions and feels he can't stop what they have started.

How does Kelly use language to represent Brian?

Brian's speech becomes more repetitive and rambling as the play continues. In Act 3, he speaks in short **clauses** – 'I found him, I found him, I found Adam'; the repeated phrases are fast-paced to get the others' attention and their childishness highlight his deteriorating sanity. He has other **characteristics** like using childish **imagery** and saying all his thoughts aloud: 'what do you think earth tastes like, do you think it tastes earthy?' While this can be comedic, his actions – like then eating the dirt – reminds the audience how traumatised he has been by his experience, and that Adam's isn't the only life that has been destroyed.

Key Quotations to Learn

BRIAN: I can't stand the way they look at me. And then, because I cry, they think I'm telling the truth, but I'm crying because I'm lying and I feel terrible inside. (2.3)

BRIAN: I wonder what earth tastes like, what do you think it ... *He bends down to eat a handful of earth.* (3.3)

Brian is giggling inside, looking around and breathing the plastic in and out of his mouth. BRIAN: Bit stuffy. (3.3)

Summary

- Brian's frequent crying is a symbol of his weakness.
- Like Adam, he is a victim of bullying by the others who control him.
- He lies when he tells the police that someone flashed him in the woods.
- Brian suffers a nervous breakdown; his language becomes repetitive and childlike.

Sample Analysis

Kelly presents Brian as weak, whose mind can't cope with the trauma of what they have done. When they find Adam he says, 'I crawled, I love crawling, I love crawling ...'. The repetition is childish, designed to get attention until he is praised for his actions. His **tone** sounds pleased with himself, as obedience has been his role in the group. However, the verb 'crawling' is a metaphor for his position of subservience within the group, and puts him in a similar position to Adam – once Adam is gone, they turn on Brian.

Questions

QUICK TEST
1. Which character in the play is Brian most like? Why?
2. What is Brian's role in the plan?
3. How does Brian change?
4. How does Brian's language change?

EXAM PRACTICE
Using one of the 'Key Quotations to Learn', write a paragraph analysing the ways that Brian could be seen as a victim.

You must be able to: analyse the way that Danny is presented, and his importance in the play.

What is Danny like?

Danny seems to be one of the more serious, **aspirational** characters. In the first scene, he says he has plans to be a dentist. He is panicking when he is first introduced as 'A levels are part of the plan; dead people are not part of the plan'. The repetition in the line creates humour despite the bleak situation.

He is slightly confrontational, asking John Tate, 'How can you ban a word?' and of Phil 'Is he serious?' Using questions to challenge makes him seem weaker; he doesn't directly confront the other characters but hedges his concerns and doesn't act on them.

What is Danny's role in the group?

Danny's contribution is minimal, carrying Jan to simulate footsteps. However, he does as instructed, showing that he is a follower who will support the group to protect his own future.

He repeats phrases related to prestige and accomplishment, like 'A levels' and 'references', which indicates how focused he is on his future. This might seem contradictory given his role in bullying Adam, but reminds the audience that not all of the group were present at Adam's 'death' and that they are all working on the cover-up regardless.

What happens to him?

Danny isn't onstage after Act 2, so he doesn't see Adam's return. His absence perhaps suggests that he has had enough and won't associate with the group but it could also be interpreted as the group now don't trust him with the secret of Adam's reappearance.

In Act 4, Richard tells Phil that Danny is doing work experience at a dentist's, but Danny's trauma is coming through, as he hates it: 'he says when they open their mouths sometimes it feels like you're going to fall in'. This **metaphor** (linking falling into mouths with Adam falling through the grille) suggests he cannot forget what happened. This represents people's difficulty dealing with trauma or suffering post-traumatic stress disorder (PTSD) when the brain can't cope with an experience but continues to try to deal with it in different ways. In Danny's case, the open mouth has become symbolic of the dark hole under the grille.

Key Quotations to Learn

DANNY: Dentists don't get involved in things. I've got a plan ... I've made plans. (1.3)

DANNY: I want to keep calm, I want to say nothing, just like you. (1.3)

DANNY: We can't let them think it's him, I mean, I really can't be mixed up in something like that, it wouldn't be right. (2.3)

Summary

- Danny is more serious and aspirational than the others.
- He knows the dangers to his future that Adam's death poses.
- He echoes the audience's disbelief at the behaviour of John and Phil.
- He is concerned about framing someone.
- He hates dentistry when he tries it, unable to overcome the traumatic image of Adam falling through the grille.

Sample Analysis

Danny functions as a reminder of those people who are motivated by self-interest at the expense of others around them. He repeats the question, 'how am I gonna get references?' Depending on the actor's tone, this might be challenging and demanding a response from the others while ignoring their conversation about the arrested postman; his irrelevant interjection could be frustrating as he's not contributing to a group solution. However, the tone could also be hopeless, a rhetorical question as he faces the ruin of his future.

Questions

QUICK TEST

1. How does Danny compare with the others?
2. What are his concerns following Adam's 'death'?
3. How does he challenge John and Phil?
4. What happens to him after Act 2?
5. How does he symbolise people's response to trauma?

EXAM PRACTICE

Using one of the 'Key Quotations to Learn', write a paragraph analysing how far Kelly presents Danny as a selfish character.

Adam

You must be able to: analyse the way Adam is presented, and his importance in the play.

What makes Adam a victim?

Mark and Jan recount the horrific events leading to Adam's apparent death, saying 'he was laughing harder than anyone'. However, they are justifying themselves so their account cannot be trusted and they might be exaggerating. Adam's experience worsens after his return. There is **pathos** as the audience realises Phil's decision to kill him makes the miracle of his reappearance worthless. It is worse too because the first 'death' is the accidental result of a sequence of events that go too far, but the second death is deliberate murder.

How does Adam seem when he returns?

He has suffered a head injury, and his speech is disorganised: 'I was new / A new / a new / a new me', showing his difficulty understanding what has happened to him. His return is a turning point in the play; rather than covering up an accidental death, some of the group now deliberately commit murder.

Why doesn't Adam come back after getting out of the grille?

He says he felt like he died: 'I saw this light and went that way ... because that's what people do'. He was living in the hedges and 'couldn't remember things'. This imagery is conflicting because the first phrase suggests that Adam has had a spiritual experience, but it is **juxtaposed** with the prosaic nature of the second phrase, which implies he's simply suffered a serious head injury. He says he 'was new' and 'And I felt / happy'. The positive language is a façade; the audience sees his physical trauma as contributing to the impression that Adam is **psychologically** damaged.

How is Adam presented through others' opinions of him?

Adam is presented as weak and a follower. Mark and Jan describe him 'hanging around', 'trying to be a part of' the group, their **colloquial** language sounding dismissive of him and portraying him as a nuisance. They take advantage of this in making him do dangerous things for 'a laugh'.

Leah is the only one directly expressing fondness for him, reminding Phil that 'we used to go to his birthday parties'. Allusion to this commonplace event creates sympathy, as she is pleading for his life by using the collective pronoun and emphasising that they've been connected since childhood. But Phil has decided Adam really must die in order to protect the group.

Key Quotations to Learn

A boy who looks like a tramp. His clothes are torn and dirty, and his hair is matted with dried blood. (3.3)

ADAM: woke, woke, woke up, I woke up with liquid on my head, leaves, dead and rotting. (3.3)

LEAH: It's Adam, Phil, Adam! We used to go to his birthday parties, he used to have that cheap ice cream and we used to take the piss, remember? (3.3)

Summary

- Adam is a victim of bullying from childhood.
- His death prompts an outpouring of grief, and people claiming they have been affected.
- He reappears in 3.3, which is a turning point in the plot.
- Phil instructs Cathy to kill Adam.
- Leah is the only one to protest against Adam's murder.

Sample Analysis

Adam's language demonstrates his trauma. He describes escaping the tunnel 'crawl, crawling in this / dark / place'. An audience already shocked is sympathetic to the horrors of his experience and the **claustrophobia** created by the repetition of 'crawl'. Kelly creates breaks between lines (/) to pause the actor's speech, suggesting Adam's fragmented understanding of what happened to him. The verb 'crawl' makes him sound childlike and frightened, particularly placed beside the **adjective** 'dark', describing his position as extremely vulnerable.

Questions

QUICK TEST
1. What makes Adam a victim?
2. How does his death affect the community?
3. What is his speech like when he returns?
4. How has he been living?

EXAM PRACTICE
Using one of the 'Key Quotations to Learn', write a paragraph analysing the ways that Adam is presented as vulnerable.

You must be able to: analyse the way that Richard and Lou are presented, and their importance in the play.

What's Richard's role in Adam's death and cover-up?

He takes Brian to the Head to identify a 'flasher'. His exclamation ('But I hate him!') with the childish verb 'hate' reflects his immaturity yet makes their lie more believable as they wouldn't naturally be together.

What is his language like?

He uses **sarcastic**, challenging put-downs ('that is the most stupid ...') to exert his superiority over others. He complains to John and Phil but ultimately follows instructions.

How does Richard change?

Richard was a leader before John arrived, as shown by John saying to him, 'I thought we'd got over all that silliness ... I thought we were mates now'. Richard is challenging but insecure (*Steps forward, a little hesitantly.* 'You shouldn't threaten me, John'). His nerves take over and he allows John to lead.

Richard demonstrates his guilt through kind actions, inviting Mark to his party and calling his dog Adam. At the end, Richard (not Leah) is in the field with Phil. He '*walks on his hands*', a physical method of entertainment to try get Phil's attention. Richard's final monologue contrasts the isolation of individuals with the huge community of the universe.

What is the significance of Lou?

Lou is a follower, acting without question. She follows instructions from John and Phil, then finally Cathy. She even accepts the lie of the cover-up completely:

> LOU: Because he saw him in the woods.
> LEAH: He didn't
> LOU: He did, he –

What is Lou's language like?

She has short simple utterances ('We're screwed') that make her seem childish, maybe younger than the others. She repeats others' phrases from earlier in the play (RICHARD: You dick, Mark / LOU: Mark, you dick'), which could be humorous but also suggests she has trouble expressing her own thoughts and follows the opinions of others.

Key Quotations to Learn

LOU: Because he's dead, John, he's dead, dead is what he is so we have to use that word to – (1.3)

LEAH: Who is he?
LOU: He's the man who kidnapped Adam. (2.3)

RICHARD: You dick, Mark. (2.3)

RICHARD: Lou's [Cathy's] best friend now. Dangerous game. I feel sorry for Lou. (4.2)

Summary

- Richard is sometimes childish, and challenges people by using sarcastic put-downs.
- He used to be a leader but becomes a follower.
- By the end, Richard seems desperate for Phil's attention.
- Lou has simple utterances that make her seem young.
- Lou is a follower, accepting the cover-up as reality despite knowing it is a lie and being part of it.

Sample Analysis

In Richard's final monologue he expresses a sense of individual isolation as he feels 'like I was an alien in a cloud', separated from his community. This **simile** suggests he is literally 'alienated' from society, cut off in the all-encompassing 'cloud' around him. Although he says that we are not alone in the universe, he is isolated at this moment as well as physically isolated in the field with Phil. The 'cloud' imagery suggests something not physical that is difficult to get hold of, subject to drifting away at the mercy of external forces, which reflects the way Richard feels he is adrift and can't connect with society.

Questions

QUICK TEST
1. How does Richard change?
2. What language does Richard use to challenge others?
3. What is Lou's role?
4. What is Lou's language like?

EXAM PRACTICE
Using one of the 'Key Quotations to Learn', write a paragraph analysing the ways that Lou or Richard is presented.

You must be able to: analyse the way that John Tate is presented, and his importance in the play.

How is John Tate presented at the beginning of the play?

John only appears in Act 1 Scene 3, when the group have gone to him for help. He seems afraid of the problem, banning the word 'dead' from the conversation although this is challenged by Lou and Danny. He struggles to find a solution, relying on clichés like 'let's not overplay the ... gravity of the situation' and downplaying the seriousness of events. However, he bluntly declares 'Dead. He's dead', when Mark hesitates and can't say the word, which suggests he could have more courage than the others – or it could create humour, as he previously banned the word and is now using it.

He sees position and power as critical, reminding them 'I am trying to keep everyone together'. He believes the group are envied by others who 'want to be us, come here in the woods'.

How does John Tate's role in the group change?

John refers to recently arriving, which suggests he has taken over leadership of the group from Richard. He makes sure Danny and Brian are on 'his side' and threatens to 'bite their face' if they don't offer verbal reassurances that they support him. However, he effectively hands over control of the situation and the group to Phil when he asks for his help because Cathy says Phil is 'clever', implying John knows he can't solve the problem himself.

What is John Tate's significance at the end?

The audience learns from Richard that John has 'found god' and is trying to convert others, perhaps to reduce his guilt for his part in Adam's death (telling the police he thought he saw Adam with someone). This could be seen as positive, turning his back on gang culture, but Richard's description could also be seen as desperation.

How does Kelly use language to show John Tate's lack of leadership?

John uses repetition ('No, no, it's not, no, Lou') showing his fragmented thought process. He uses fragmented utterances ('I'm not trying to hide the, this is tricky, it's a tricky'), representing his difficulty in controlling the situation. His language is often cautious. He says the word dead is 'banned. Sorry' and 'I'm gonna hurt you, actually'. The words 'sorry' and 'actually' are hedges, softening his authority and making him sound uncertain and less confident.

Key Quotations to Learn

JOHN TATE: Ever since I came to this school haven't I been trying to keep everyone together? ... Doesn't everyone want to be us, come here in the woods? Isn't that worth keeping hold of? (1.3)

JOHN TATE: Because if you've got a side that means you're not on my side and if you're not on my side that means you're setting yourself up against me. (1.3)

Summary

- John only appears in Act 1 Scene 3, as leader of the group.
- He seems to have taken control from Richard, but then hands control to Phil by asking for a plan.
- He rules through fear and violence and believes that power and being envied are important.
- At the end he has 'found god', suggesting he seeks forgiveness. However, this could indicate his desperation.

Sample Analysis

John is a weak leader who relies on others' fear and passivity to maintain his position. His speech is filled with clichés – 'We have to keep together. We have to trust each other and believe in each other.' The repeated use of the plural pronoun emphasises the group dynamic he is trying to preserve, and the **parallelism** of the verbs 'trust' and 'believe' are positive and inspiring. But in Tate's hesitant speech, they don't sound sincere; instead, they merely sound as though they are what he thinks he should say.

Questions

QUICK TEST
1. When does John Tate appear?
2. How does he react initially to Adam's death?
3. How does he try to keep control?
4. What has happened to him by the end?

EXAM PRACTICE
Using one of the 'Key Quotations to Learn', write a paragraph analysing the significance of John Tate's character.

You must be able to: analyse the way that Kelly explores ideas about bullying.

How does Kelly present physical bullying?

Physical bullying is directed towards Adam and Brian, the weaker characters. The characters describe bullying Adam, including making him eat 'big fistfuls of leaves', which escalates to torture as they 'stubbed out cigarettes on him'. They use everyday objects to inflict harm on Adam, and use colloquial language to describe what they do to him, making the bullying more disturbing, with shockingly physical brutality conveyed through simple phrasing.

Most of Adam's bullying is offstage, described by Mark and Jan to the group. Mark takes delight in describing their power over Adam: 'you had to laugh, the expression, the fear'. This list of emotions demonstrates the bullies' callous response as they torment Adam. Kelly presents shame in Mark's description, including line breaks and additional punctuation to create hesitation: 'And he drops. / Into … / Into the er … /'.

How does Kelly present psychological bullying?

John Tate and Phil bully psychologically, including threatening others. John insists others swear allegiance to 'his side' to keep power and threatens them if they challenge him. The language of 'sides' is immature but represents how people obtain power by having the support of those around them. Others, including Danny and Brian, are psychologically bullied as they are threatened by John, who threatens violence, and Phil, who threatens to kill Brian if he doesn't support the cover-up.

Phil emotionally bullies Leah, by ignoring her appeals for attention. ('Do I disgust you? I do.') She threatens to leave and 'strangles herself' until she 'is in considerable pain' to get his attention. However, Leah has also been involved in bullying, 'taking the piss' out of Adam for cheap ice cream at his birthday parties. Thus, Kelly questions whether even 'low level' bullying is forgivable.

The effects of bullying

Adam's death is a result of a series of actions which, individually, are viewed by the teenagers as insignificant, even comical, but which are seen in hindsight as a chain of events leading to his death. Kelly is warning audiences about taking these bullying actions lightly. Other characters' lives are destroyed or forever altered. Leah, a victim of emotional bullying, becomes unhappier until she eventually leaves her relationship with Phil and the rest of the group. Brian's psychological bullying combined with the guilt of Adam's death leads to his insanity.

Key Quotations to Learn

MARK: And someone's pegged a stone at him. (1.3)

PHIL: You have to go in. Or we'll take you up the grille. *Pause.* We'll throw you in. (2.3)

CATHY: If you don't shut up you'll be dead. (3.3)

Summary

- Kelly presents physical and psychological/emotional bullying.
- Bullying preys on weaker characters like Brian and Adam.
- Most of the physical bullying is offstage, making the audience imagine it.
- Psychological bullying particularly affects Danny, Brian and Leah.
- Most characters have engaged in bullying, including Leah.

Sample Analysis

Kelly explores the worst consequences of bullying when Mark describes throwing stones 'getting nearer and nearer. And one hits his head. And the shock on his face is so … funny.' The **syndetic** nature of the list suggests the connection between the actions, implying that one necessarily leads to the next, portraying Adam's death as the inevitable consequence of a chain of actions. The short utterance 'And one hits his head' is a shocking turning point, where the characters' laughter becomes crueller, directed at someone clearly terrified. When Mark pauses, the audience will anticipate his next word and will be surprised and angered when it is 'funny', as this likely contrasts with their expectation. The pause might also represent his shame at having felt this way.

Questions

QUICK TEST

1. What types of bullying are presented?
2. Who are the main victims of bullying?
3. Why do characters like Mark and Jan bully?
4. How is Leah involved in bullying?

EXAM PRACTICE

Using one or more of the 'Key Quotations to Learn', write a paragraph analysing the ways that Kelly presents psychological and physical bullying.

Cruelty and Violence

You must be able to: analyse the way that Kelly presents ideas about violence and cruelty.

How does Kelly represent violence in the characters' language?

Many characters casually refer to violence, even apart from their direct threats, showing how common it is. In her melodramatic monologue, Leah exclaims to Phil 'So kill me, Phil, call the police, lock me up, rip out my teeth with a pair of rusty pliers'. Later she reveals she has killed her pet. This shocking violence is treated as difficult to understand – she doesn't know why she did it and she simply discards the dead body.

Other characters use violence to threaten, including Phil, Cathy and John towards Brian.

How does violence develop through the play?

The violence increases, becoming more deliberate and calculating, developing into cruelty because of the perpetrators' lack of concern for their victims.

The cruelty in Adam's torture before the play could be seen as developing spontaneously, a series of events that are less deliberate because they are not planned. Mark describes asking Adam 'just to see' if he can climb over the grille. When Mark slips into second person ('you're having a laugh together'), this implies he's distancing himself from the violent actions, suggesting that anybody could feel this way.

Phil and Cathy's planned murder of Adam seems more violent because of its calculated nature. The language describing it is less explicit as Phil says 'If he comes back our lives are ruined. He can't come back, Cathy'. The visual instruction is graphic, in contrast with the offstage cruelty described in Act 1.

Who are the cruellest characters?

Cathy shows the most development towards cruelty. At first, she is excited by Adam's death ('Better than ordinary life') but might not have been directly involved. By the time he reappears she has become routinely violent, threatening to 'gouge his eyes out' to make him come down from the hedge he's been living in. In Act 4 Richard says she has 'cut a first year's finger off'.

Phil also becomes crueller. When Phil plans the cover-up, his tone is matter-of-fact, but this could be because he is protecting the group. But later he argues for Adam's death by asking 'are you happy?' when it is evident Adam is in no state to respond, and Phil's question is self-serving. Phil is the most visually violent onstage, putting a plastic bag on Brian's head 'making it airtight', foreshadowing the offstage action Cathy will carry out.

Key Quotations to Learn

JAN: Stubbed out cigarettes on him ... Arms, hands, face ... soles of his feet (1.3)

LEAH: [Chimps] kill and sometimes torture each other to find a better position within the social structure. (2.3)

BRIAN: She was gonna do it [gouge out Adam's eye]. She loves violence now. (3.3)

Summary

- Leah and others use violent language routinely – it is part of their everyday lives.
- Violence becomes more calculating through the play, escalating to cruelty.
- Cathy changes most to become the cruellest character, using violence to control others.
- Phil acts cruelly when planning Adam's murder, but claims he does this for the good of the group.

Sample Analysis

When Leah describes killing her hamster her language is blunt and direct: 'I put the point of a screwdriver on his head and I hit it with a hammer'. At this point, Leah is perceived as less violent, so this is even more unexpectedly brutal. The mundane nouns 'screwdriver' and 'hammer' perpetuate the impression that violence is an everyday occurrence. She asks, 'why do you think I did that?', the rhetorical question revealing the way that the characters feel caught up in events beyond their control or understanding.

Questions

QUICK TEST
1. How does Kelly show violence through language?
2. How does Mark distance himself from the violence of their actions?
3. How does violence develop into cruelty?
4. Who is the cruellest character?

EXAM PRACTICE
Using one or more of the 'Key Quotations to Learn', write a paragraph analysing the ways that cruelty is presented.

Science and Religion

You must be able to: analyse the way that Kelly explores ideas about science and religion.

How does Kelly present ideas about science?

The title refers to modern society's reliance on the dependability of scientific methods but the DNA evidence is planted, so the findings are unreliable. Gathering DNA from someone who fits the invented description means that the police don't look elsewhere. Phil's plan shows an understanding of other scientific investigation methods. However, all the 'evidence' is fabricated, which suggests that science should be used carefully and critically because it can be manipulated to indicate an untruth.

Where else are scientific references present?

Other social institutions are associated with science. Leah mentions the school's 'even naming the science lab after him, for god's sake', in a curious juxtaposition of science and spirituality, using the lab as a memorial. However, the use of 'god' is colloquial, that is, it is not intended to have genuine religious **connotations** but rather merely to indicate disbelief.

Characters such as Danny and Brian are associated with science; Danny wants to be a dentist, and Brian is subject to medical intervention as he's on 'stronger and stronger medication' and at risk of being sectioned. Ultimately, neither association with science is positive.

How is Leah associated with science?

Leah's monologues often begin with scientific ideas. Her description of the difference between chimps and bonobos illustrates humans' different behaviours. When talking about happiness, she uses different planets' environments to explore the fragility of life.

How does Kelly use religious symbolism?

Adam's description of his death has connotations of religious ideas about heaven. He describes going towards a light and thinking that he has died. He appears to think he is dead when speaking to them. The eventual murder of Adam could also be interpreted as a **primitive** sacrifice, the killing of an individual to protect the group.

Does religion help characters cope?

At the end we learn John Tate has joined the 'Jesus Army', a Christian movement. Richard's description of him running 'round the shopping centre' and 'singing and trying to give people leaflets' sounds ineffective, perhaps implying that John Tate has 'found god' in desperation and is unsuccessfully trying to heal himself. However, this could also be Richard making the activities sound pointless, as their actions are, ultimately, unforgivable.

Key Quotations to Learn

LEAH: They need fibres, they need samples, they need evidence.
RICHARD: DNA evidence. (2.3)

ADAM: I saw this light and went that way, towards, and I thought I died because that's what people / go to the light (3.3)

Summary

- The cover-up involves understanding of science and methods of police investigation.
- The planting of the DNA shows how science can be manipulated.
- Leah's monologues often use scientific ideas to explore the themes of the play.
- Adam describes his death using religious symbolism.
- Adam's murder could be considered a primitive sacrifice of the individual for the protection of the many.

Sample Analysis

In Leah's monologue on happiness she describes the earth in broadly scientific terms: 'When this planet is churning molten lava with a thin layer of crust on top with a few kilometres of atmosphere clinging to it?' (2.2) This imagery explores the fragility of humanity because the **determiner** 'few' reminds the audience how little of the universe is inhabitable (she also refers to other, inhospitable, planets) and how precarious humanity's life on earth is. This reflects Adam's death, suggesting it is relatively meaningless in the scale of mankind's existence.

Questions

QUICK TEST
1. How does Leah connect with science?
2. How does Kelly suggest conclusions based on science can be inaccurate?
3. Which other characters are associated with science?
4. How is Adam connected to religion?
5. How does Kelly present religion in relation to John Tate?

EXAM PRACTICE
Using one or more of the 'Key Quotations to Learn', write a paragraph analysing the ways that Kelly presents the contrast between science and religion in the play.

Leadership

You must be able to: analyse the way that Kelly presents ideas about different ways to be a leader.

How is John Tate presented as a leader?

In Act 1, John Tate is a weak leader who dominates by bullying. He alludes to taking control from Richard ('I thought we'd got over all that silliness') and intimidating others at school. His leadership fails when he turns to Leah and Phil as they are 'clever', implicitly admitting his inability to solve the problem of Adam's death. His disappearance after Act 1 could be perceived as a lack of loyalty to the group. Kelly uses John Tate to suggest that leadership based on intimidation is vulnerable.

How could Phil be described as a Machiavellian leader?

A **Machiavellian** leader is **manipulative**, keeping secrets. Phil is clever but refuses to listen to others. When the police arrest someone, the group turn to Phil for advice (LEAH: 'Everyone calm, okay. Isn't that right, Phil ...') but he lets Cathy explain. This could indicate he is listening closely or could show his lack of interest.

Is Phil a good leader?

Initially, Phil's plan protects the group, accepting that Adam is dead so they should now save themselves. Cathy and Mark 'show initiative', suggesting they want to impress Phil. He tells Cathy 'our lives will be ruined' if Adam returns; using the plural implies his group loyalty.

Phil becomes a weaker leader, resorting to violence. He brutally threatens Brian, saying 'We'll take you up the grille ... We'll throw you in'. He doesn't listen to Leah, despite her reputation for being clever.

How does Cathy become a leader?

At first Cathy is a follower. She causes trouble by telling John there are 'sides'. By the time she gets DNA evidence 'it was her idea' to 'show initiative' by framing a real postman. She successfully leads through violence; she suddenly slaps Brian, and proudly states 'I used violence' to get Adam to come back.

Phil and Cathy understand one another when discussing Adam's murder:

> PHIL: Make a game of it...
> CATHY: How?

Her question implies she is keen to learn from Phil, even when it comes to murder. In Act 4 she is 'running things', using rumours and gossip to fuel fear and to keep people in line.

How far is Leah a positive view of leadership?

Leah tries to lead in a moral way and others turn to her, for example, when the police find the DNA evidence. Her lack of confidence, however, means she is weak and she turns to Phil to resolve the situation.

Key Quotations to Learn

JOHN: Everyone respects you and everyone's scared of you and who made that, I mean, I'm not boasting but who made that happen? (1.3)

PHIL: Any questions? *They stare at him, open-mouthed.* (1.3)

PHIL: We need your help. If you don't help us we'll kill you. Are you going to help us? (2.3)

Summary

- John Tate is a poor leader, using bullying and intimidation.
- His disappearance suggests that this kind of leadership will fail.
- Phil could be considered a Machiavellian leader, calculating and secretive.
- He uses cruelty and threats to keep the others in line.
- Cathy changes from a follower to a leader, also leading through violence.

Sample Analysis

Kelly presents Cathy as a leader by the end when she has 'cut a first year's finger off, that's what they say anyway'. The casual tone of 'anyway' highlights the everyday way in which Cathy seems to inflict violence after murdering Adam. The phrase 'they say' introduces doubt, showing she is using rumours to intimidate others into being afraid and following her.

Questions

QUICK TEST
1. What kind of a leader is John Tate?
2. What similarities in leadership are shown by Phil and John Tate?
3. How is Phil effective as a leader?
4. How does Cathy's leadership develop?
5. What kind of a leader is Leah?

EXAM PRACTICE
Using one or more of the 'Key Quotations to Learn', write a paragraph analysing the different ways that Kelly presents leadership.

Death

You must be able to: analyse the way that Kelly presents ideas about death in the play.

How does Kelly present the first 'death'?

Mark and Jan's stichomythia at first makes death seem comical. 'Living dead' is a reminder of the ubiquity of death in modern media but presented in a way that removes it from reality. Their duologue becomes less comic through the act until the audience realise Adam has been bullied to death (although unintended), and that the characters enjoyed it until the last moment. Mark and Jan can't admit their responsibility, instead trailing off:

MARK: So he's ... So he's ... So he's ...
JOHN TATE: Dead. He's dead.

Both the bullying of Adam that is described and his first 'death' occur offstage. This could reduce empathy for him because he's unknown to the audience,

How does the theme of death change by Act 3?

Phil's instruction to Cathy is a visual demonstration of murder as he *'puts a plastic bag over Brian's head'*. This action is onstage but the death itself is again offstage, which reflects the hidden nature of it and the need for secrecy. The second death echoes the first as it is a repetition of the action (the death), but is different because it is now deliberate murder, rather than accidental death.

Adam's reappearance means that the audience has seen him now, so has more empathy for him. He is traumatised and incapacitated, which makes the situation crueller, especially since Phil's decision to murder him makes his initial survival pointless.

How does Kelly explore the impact of death on others?

Primarily through Leah, Kelly explores people's **rituals** of grief. Leah says that grief is 'pouring into the school, grief, and grief is making them happy'. She describes the impact of Adam's death on the community with babies (and dogs) being named after him, those involved 'actually behaving better', more kind and generous to others. At the memorial 'everyone felt wonderful. It's incredible' how people have come together in mourning.

However, Leah's speech also satirises the way that some people exploit death. Cathy is 'on every channel' after being interviewed. Leah bitterly comments that 'suddenly Adam's everyone's best friend' when it seems clear to the audience that Adam was abandoned or victimised by most of the people around him.

Key Quotations to Learn

PHIL: They'll be inquiries, police, mourning, a service and if everyone keeps their mouths shut we should be fine. (1.3)

ADAM: I thought I died because that's what people / go to the light, you / and there was such a pain in my / I thought the light would make it go ... (3.3)

PHIL: He's dead. everyone thinks he's dead. What difference will it make?
She stares at him.
LEAH: But he's not dead. He's alive. (3.3)

Summary

- Adam's first 'death' is brutal and violent but accidental.
- The second – real – death is crueller because it is deliberate.
- Leah's conversations with Phil explore rituals of grief people use to move on.
- Leah is sarcastic about people's hypocrisy in claiming to have been friends with Adam.

Sample Analysis

Kelly explores rituals surrounding grief when Leah exclaims 'but there's been a service, there's been appeals, there's been weeping ... They're naming the science lab after him, for god's sake'. Her list of actions echoes Phil's earlier list; the activities are designed to create closure but are also public symbols of mourning that might become performances. Her exclamation 'for god's sake' sounds exasperated, as though Adam's return is a frustration of these efforts.

Questions

QUICK TEST
1. How does Kelly make death seem brutal?
2. What are the echoes between Adam's two deaths?
3. How does Leah describe people's responses to death?

EXAM PRACTICE
Using one or more of the 'Key Quotations to Learn', write a paragraph analysing the different impacts of death.

You must be able to: analyse the way that Kelly presents ideas about alienation.

What is alienation?

Alienation is a sense of feeling isolated from one's community, feeling that you don't have common values, morals or beliefs.

How are the characters presented as being alienated from society?

The settings reflect their isolation, becoming increasingly private in each act (wood, field). Even the streets are isolated from other people.

Social institutions (schools, police, the media) are on the fringes of the play, suggesting the characters don't feel connected to them. They can be manipulated, like the police (with the false DNA trail) or the school (when Brian reports the 'flasher').

The characters see these institutions as punitive (punishing), not supportive. Phil says 'our lives are ruined' if they are discovered. Although Danny, Brian and Leah suggest telling 'someone', they aren't specific, indicating they don't know who to tell. The police are presented as an obstacle to their futures. School is a place where the *effects* of Adam's death are seen ('grief is pouring into the school', 'they're naming the science lab after him') but with little impact on the teenagers. Using language like 'they' and 'someone' reflects the distance between the characters and these institutions.

How are the characters alienated from social values?

Although they initially believe Adam is dead, they are not yet entirely alienated from social values – they cover it up to escape punishment, knowing his 'death' is wrong. Some characters return to society, like John Tate after the initial plan, and Lou when Adam returns. Phil and Cathy's decision to kill Adam demonstrates their total alienation from society – not committing murder is a basic rule of civilisation.

How are the characters presented as being alienated from each other?

John Tate describes them as separate from everyone else: 'doesn't everyone want to be us, come here in the woods?' His statement that 'we have to trust each other' also seems **ironic**; alliances form and shift, and by the end they have all separated. They gradually leave one another, starting with John who disappears after Act 1.

Act 4's structure highlights their isolation. Separate scenes with Mark/Jan, then Phil/Richard imply that the group is not unified any more.

Key Quotations to Learn

LEAH: I couldn't say this to anyone else, they'd say 'that's a pretty bloody grim view of the world, Leah'. (2.1)

LEAH: Your brain is entirely waffle, single-mindedly waffle and maybe a bit of jam, I don't know how you do it. I admire you so much. (3.2)

RICHARD: I knew we weren't alone in the universe ... But I couldn't see who they were or what they were doing or how they were living. (4.2)

Summary

- Alienation means feeling isolated from a community, without common values or beliefs.
- The characters see social institutions (police, education, media) as tools to be manipulated or avoided.
- They see these institutions as likely to punish rather than support them.
- The settings and structure reflect their isolation, including from one another.

Sample Analysis

Leah wonders if being together has made people happier, removing their sense of alienation, 'having something to work towards. Together ... Are we really that simple?' The 'simple' adjective implies that she thinks that there should be something more complex about community. Kelly isolates the word 'together', indicating a pause in the actor's delivery as though trying to understand the concept of society. In contrast, Leah is often in isolated places, particularly the field, where she is not connected with anyone.

Questions

QUICK TEST
1. What does alienation mean?
2. How do the teenagers view social institutions?
3. How do the settings reflect their isolation?
4. How does the play's structure present their alienation?
5. How are they alienated from one another?

EXAM PRACTICE
Using one or more of the 'Key Quotations to Learn', write a paragraph analysing the ways that Kelly presents his characters as alienated from society.

Morality

You must be able to: analyse the way that Kelly presents the theme of morality.

How does Kelly view morality in his play?

Kelly has said that although there is a 'moral centre' to his play, it is 'asking a moral question, and probably one that I don't have the answer to'. Morality (understanding what is right and wrong) conventionally suggests that murder is wrong. However, covering up the first 'murder' could be seen as acceptable because it has already happened, and the characters are struggling to save their own futures. The second, though, reminds an audience that murder is usually considered a moral absolute (an action that is *always* wrong).

Who could be considered amoral or immoral characters?

An immoral person knows right from wrong and behaves in a way they know is wrong. An amoral person does not distinguish between right and wrong.

Cathy could be interpreted as an amoral character; she makes trouble to see the consequences ('He's on Richard's side') and acts in her own interests until at the end she is 'running things'.

Phil could be considered to be immoral; he invents the cover-up and progresses to ordering Adam's death. However, he sees himself as moral. He *'smiles kindly. Nods'* when Adam says he wants to go back, as though he is doing the right thing by letting Adam decide. When he explains to Leah 'Everyone's happier. What's more important, one person or everyone?' it seems he believes that sacrificing Adam is the right thing to do for the good of everyone else.

All the characters behave immorally by helping to cover up Adam's death.

Who could be considered moral characters?

Several characters could be seen as more moral, including Lou, Jan, Mark, Brian, Richard, John Tate and Danny. They aren't directly involved in murdering Adam and have minor roles in the cover-up. By the end the group has become distant from one another, either by choice or, in Brian's case, his loss of sanity.

Leah could be the most moral character as she most obviously contradicts Phil ('But he isn't dead. He's alive') and argues for Adam's life. However, her monologues suggest she isn't completely moral, for example, pointlessly killing her hamster with a screwdriver.

Key Quotations to Learn

LEAH: He won't get done for it because he hasn't …
DANNY: This sort of stuff sticks, you know. (2.3)

LEAH: Where did you get the DNA evidence?
CATHY: From a man, like you said.
Beat.
A man down at the sorting office.
LEAH: Yes. We might actually be … This is a nightmare. (2.3)

Summary

- Morality is concerned with understanding the difference between right and wrong.
- Immorality is shown by someone choosing to behave in a way they know is wrong; amorality is not caring about the difference between right and wrong.
- Kelly says the play has a moral centre and asks moral questions.
- Leah could be considered a moral character for challenging Phil but she does some immoral things.
- Phil could be seen as immoral and Cathy could be seen as amoral.

Sample Analysis

In Leah's final scene with Phil she accepts the sweet then '*Suddenly she stops chewing and spits the sweet out'*. This action is a physical rejection of Phil and his sense of morality. Taking the sweet symbolises her temptation to accept what has happened. Spitting it out is a violent rejection, foreshadowing the next scene where the audience learns she has left the school, turning her back on the group and its immorality.

Questions

QUICK TEST
1. How does Kelly view the play's morality?
2. Who are the most moral characters?
3. Who are the most immoral or amoral characters?
4. Are there any purely moral characters?

EXAM PRACTICE
Using one or more of the 'Key Quotations to Learn', write a paragraph analysing the way that Kelly presents one of his characters as a moral force.

Responsibility

You must be able to: analyse the way that Kelly presents ideas about responsibility in the play.

How does Kelly represent personal responsibility surrounding Adam's bullying?

Individuals justify their actions, as Mark and Jan describe Adam 'laughing' during their torture. Jan says she 'went home' before he fell into the grille.

Leah and Phil are told onstage about his death, showing the audience they weren't directly involved, but Mark uses the collective pronoun 'we' and uses no names, making personal responsibility unclear. Nobody accepts personal responsibility for what they have done to Adam.

How does Kelly represent collective responsibility?

By participating in the cover-up, they all have collective responsibility, defined as being responsible for others' actions by ignoring or tolerating them.

When planning Adam's death, Phil tells Lou, Mark and Jan 'if you go now and you say nothing to no one about this, you won't be in trouble.' This is both a threat and reassurance: if they ignore his solution, they won't get in trouble but they will if they go to the authorities.

How does Kelly use structure to show characters who are less responsible?

John and Danny disappear mid-way through the play, having separated themselves from the group. They aren't seen again. They remain unaware of Adam's reappearance so aren't responsible for murder.

Brian's mental decline through the play means he isn't responsible for the murder. Although he knows Adam is alive and goes with Cathy to kill him, he thinks it's to 'play a game'. Phil calls the plastic bag 'an experiment' and Brian is delighted, suggesting he doesn't understand what is about to happen. He is clearly suffering from a mental breakdown by this point. His inability to make logical, rational decisions makes him less responsible.

Why does Kelly explore collective responsibility?

By encouraging the audience to consider whether the teenagers are justified in safeguarding their futures at Adam's expense, Kelly asks them to consider whether they too hold collective responsibility by accepting first the cover-up and then the murder.

Key Quotations to Learn

LEAH: [If] we have done a thing, which we haven't, but if we have then we did it together. (1.3)

PHIL: We've got this situation. It wasn't supposed to be like this. But it is like this. (2.4)

LEAH: You know, omelettes and eggs, as long as you've your waffle, who cares? (3.2)

Summary

- Kelly explores two types of responsibility: personal and collective.
- Nobody accepts personal responsibility. Mark uses 'we' to obscure the identities of those involved in Adam's torture.
- All characters hold collective responsibility as they ignore or tolerate the bullying, cover-up and murder.
- John Tate and Danny are not responsible for the murder. Brian can also be seen as not responsible as his mental state means he's incapable of understanding it.

Sample Analysis

Phil doesn't accept personal responsibility. When Adam returns, Phil tells Leah 'he's dead. Everyone thinks he's dead. What difference will it make?' His repetition of dead, from the concrete 'he <u>is</u>' to the conceptual 'everyone <u>thinks</u>' shows he sees the difference between them as **semantic** rather than significant. He asks a rhetorical question – he doesn't care what Leah says because he has already made his decision. By making and justifying this decision, Phil refuses to take the second chance to accept responsibility for Adam's disappearance as it would mean having to deal with the consequences.

Questions

QUICK TEST
1. What types of responsibility are explored?
2. Who is personally responsible for Adam's initial disappearance?
3. Who is collectively responsible for it?
4. Who is personally responsible for Adam's murder?
5. Who might be argued as being less responsible for Adam's murder?

EXAM PRACTICE
Using one or more of the 'Key Quotations to Learn', write a paragraph analysing the way that Kelly presents his characters as being morally responsible.

Gangs and Loyalty

You must be able to: analyse the way that Kelly presents ideas about gangs and loyalty.

How does Kelly present being in a gang?

The characters all want to belong, finding comfort in togetherness. Gangs typically have a strong leader and a clear hierarchy. Leadership shifts from John to Phil because of a warped sense of strength. John loses the leadership as he seems less confident, whereas Phil seems certain.

Kelly uses inclusive language to emphasise belonging. John Tate repeatedly refers to 'us' and 'everyone' else, showing their alienation and the deep divisions between them and society. This reinforces their desire to feel a sense of belonging, but also makes them reliant on each other. The characters repeatedly ask, 'what are <u>we</u> going to do?', indicating they feel they are acting as a unit.

The gang's ties are weak; they break apart. Leah depicts their isolation even from one another as she says: 'I could walk out of here, there are friends, I've got … I mean alright, I haven't got friends, not exactly'. Although they are together, they don't necessarily consider themselves as friends.

Which characters show loyalty?

Leah is loyal to Phil most of the time, shown in her constant presence, her concern for his welfare and her desire to know his thoughts. She turns to him first, despite her own intelligence, relying on him to lead the gang. Her departure at the end reflects her realisation that their loyalty to one another has led to murder.

Lou is loyal to Cathy. At the end she is 'Cathy's best friend', which is a 'dangerous game'. However, Lou changes allegiances quickly, so her loyalty is questionable.

Richard is the most loyal, flattering Phil by saying, 'wasn't it good when Phil was running the show?'

Who are the least loyal characters?

John Tate and Danny disappear mid-way through the play; neither are mentioned again, which could suggest either they've separated themselves or have been abandoned by the gang, perhaps as self-preservation for those still in it.

Phil's plans – the cover-up and murder – could signal loyalty to the gang, solving their problems. However, he doesn't participate in any actions himself directly but manipulates others into action. In the final scene he 'says nothing … staring at nothing', refusing to acknowledge Richard, and has left the gang behind.

Key Quotations to Learn

JOHN: [Then] you're on your own side, which is very, well, to be honest, very silly and dangerous. (1.3)

LEAH: A chimp'll just find itself on the outside of the group and before he knows what's happening it's being hounded to death. (1.4)

LOU: What about ... what about Cathy? (3.3)

Summary

- Gangs have strong leaders and hierarchies, with followers doing as they are told.
- The gang's loyalties aren't strong, shifting allegiances to different people.
- Although Leah is loyal to Phil for most of the play, Richard could ultimately be seen as most loyal.
- John and Danny leave mid-way through the play, perhaps showing their self-interest and preservation.
- Phil might be the least loyal as he leaves them after Adam's murder, having manipulated them all the way through.

Sample Analysis

Kelly presents the loyalty of the gang from the beginning when John Tate turns to Phil and Leah and asks 'So. What do we do? *Pause*.' Although Phil and Leah didn't actually participate in the offstage death of Adam, John's use of 'we' signifies his confidence that they won't tell the authorities and will be supportive of the rest of the gang who caused Adam's death. His blunt **discourse marker** 'So.' with an indicated pause also suggests his confidence that their support is guaranteed.

Questions

QUICK TEST
1. What are the characteristics of a gang?
2. What language initially creates a sense of loyalty?
3. Which characters show loyalty?
4. Who are the least loyal characters?

EXAM PRACTICE
Using one or more of the 'Key Quotations to Learn', explain how Kelly presents at least one of his characters as loyal.

You must be able to: analyse the way that Kelly presents ideas about happiness.

How does Leah present happiness?

Leah's monologues reveal her insecurities. Rhetorically asking Phil 'are you happy?' explores ideas about people's need to *appear* happy, suggesting that people pretend, anxious to fulfil other's expectations of what 'happy' looks like.

Kelly undercuts the potential seriousness of this moment with Leah's 'happiest moment. Week last Tuesday. That sunset.' The punctuation creates pauses which, between 'moment' and 'week', can effectively create comedy, particularly with the proximity of 'last Tuesday' to the current time. The 'sunset' is a cliché, a romanticised moment, particularly implying she watched it with Phil.

What makes people in the play happy?

Ironically, grief makes people happy. Leah explains how the community has found peace, coming together to mourn Adam, with 'everyone working together' and 'something to work towards. Together.' The sense of belonging and collaboration brings happiness.

How does Kelly suggest that happiness is difficult to understand or achieve?

When Adam returns Phil argues 'I'm in charge. Everyone is happier.' The short clauses connect to imply a causal relationship, yet it seems to an audience that the reverse is true: the happiness Leah described previously is only a temporary response to Adam's death.

Phil asks Adam if he's 'happy' under the hedge. The question is manipulative – it is in the group's best interests for Adam to stay there. The audience, though, sees his state as mentally disturbed by his trauma. Phil manipulates ideas of happiness to justify himself: if Adam is happy staying in the hedge, then to Phil it doesn't matter if he is murdered because society will not know any differently. Leah draws on happy memories ('We used to go to his birthday parties') to try to connect Phil's humanity with Adam.

Ultimately, several characters are unhappy. Danny and Brian suffer mental torment, and John Tate turns to religion.

At the end, several offstage characters could be happy depending on the audience's interpretation – it is ambiguous because we don't see them. Leah has disappeared to a new school for a fresh start. Mark and Jan are successfully shoplifting, while Cathy and Lou are successful in controlling the school, so have power which could make them happy – at least for now. Kelly has suggested that leading through violence doesn't generate longstanding happiness.

Key Quotations to Learn

LEAH: We're all supposed to be happy, happy is our natural ... (2.2)

LEAH: You have to pretend to be even happier which doesn't work because people can see that you're pretending ... (2.2)

LEAH: [Grief], grief is making them happy. (2.1)

PHIL: He's happy.
LEAH: He's not happy, he's mad. (3.3)

Summary

- Leah suggests that happiness is often a pretence or an illusion.
- She implies that people sometimes feel anxious about needing to feel happy.
- Grief makes people happier in the play because it increases their sense of belonging.
- Phil connects Adam's happiness with insanity, making happiness seem difficult to achieve.
- Some characters are unhappy at the end; it is ambiguous whether others are happy.

Sample Analysis

Leah's descriptions of happiness demonstrate its vulnerability. Speaking to Phil she describes life as 'the incredibly precious beauty and fragility of reality, and ... happiness'. Her **elevated** language suggests she values happiness but sees it as precarious. The comparison of 'happiness' with 'reality' subverts both ideas; the characters have manipulated reality by the cover-up, and in doing so, have destroyed their own hopes of happiness. The descriptions 'precious' and fragility' create pathos as it's clear that Leah is mourning something they have all lost.

Questions

QUICK TEST
1. How does Leah describe happiness?
2. How does Leah suggest happiness is an illusion?
3. How does grief make people happier in the play?
4. How does Kelly suggest happiness is difficult to understand or achieve?
5. Are any characters happy at the end?

EXAM PRACTICE
Using one or more of the 'Key Quotations to Learn', write a paragraph analysing the ways that Kelly presents happiness as an illusion.

Tips and Assessment Objectives

You must be able to: understand how to approach the exam question and meet the requirements of the mark scheme.

Quick tips

- You will get a choice of two questions. Do the one that best matches your knowledge, the quotations you have learned and the things you have revised.

- Make sure you know what the question is asking you. Underline key words and pay attention to the bullet point prompts that come with the question.

- You should spend about 45 minutes on your *DNA* response. Allow yourself five minutes to plan your answer so there is some structure to your essay.

- All your paragraphs should contain a clear idea, a relevant reference to the play (ideally a quotation) and analysis of how Kelly conveys this idea. Whenever possible, you should link your comments to the play's contexts.

- It can sometimes help, after each paragraph, to quickly re-read the question to keep yourself focused on the exam task.

- Keep your writing concise. If you waste time 'waffling' you won't be able to include the full range of analysis and understanding that the mark scheme requires.

- It is a good idea to remember what the mark scheme is asking of you.

AO1: Understand and respond to the play (12 marks)

This is all about coming up with a range of points that match the question, supporting your ideas with references from the play and writing your essay in a mature, academic style.

Lower	Middle	Upper
The essay has some good ideas that are mostly relevant. Some quotations and references are used to support the ideas.	A clear essay that always focuses on the exam question. Quotations and references support ideas effectively. The response refers to different points in the play.	A convincing, well-structured essay that answers the question fully. Quotations and references are well chosen and integrated into sentences. The response covers the whole play (not everything, but ideas from different points of the story rather than just focusing on one or two sections).

AO2: Analyse effects of Kelly's language, form and structure (12 marks)

You need to comment on how specific words, language techniques, sentence structures or the narrative structure allow Kelly to get his ideas across to the audience. This could simply be something about a character or a larger idea he is exploring through the play. To achieve this, you will need to have learned good quotations to analyse.

Lower	Middle	Upper
Identification of some different methods used by Kelly to convey meaning. Some subject terminology.	Explanation of Kelly's different methods. Clear understanding of the effects of these methods. Accurate use of subject terminology.	Analysis of the full range of Kelly's methods, including how these come across onstage. Thorough exploration of the effects of these methods. Accurate range of subject terminology.

AO3: Understand the relationship between the play and its contexts (6 marks)

For this part of the mark scheme, you need to show your understanding of how the characters or Kelly's ideas relate to the time in which he was writing (2008).

Lower	Middle	Upper
Some awareness of how ideas in the play link to its context.	References to relevant aspects of the play's context show a clear understanding.	Exploration is linked to specific aspects of the play's contexts to show a detailed understanding.

AO4: Written accuracy (4 marks)

You need to use accurate vocabulary, expression, punctuation and spelling. Although it's only 4 marks, this could make the difference between a lower or a higher grade.

Lower	Middle	Upper
Reasonable level of accuracy. Errors do not get in the way of the essay making sense.	Good level of accuracy. Vocabulary and sentences help to keep ideas clear.	Consistent high level of accuracy. Vocabulary and sentences are used to make ideas clear and precise.

1. How far does Kelly present Leah as a moral character?

   Write about:

   - some of the ways that Kelly presents the character of Leah
   - the way Kelly uses the character of Leah to present some of his ideas.

2. How far does Kelly present Phil as being in control through the play?

   Write about:

   - some of the ways that Phil is in control
   - the way Kelly presents these ideas by the ways he writes.

3. 'John Tate is a largely irrelevant character.'

   Write about:

   - the importance of John Tate in the play as a whole
   - the way Kelly presents these ideas by the ways he writes.

4. What do you think is the significance of Mark and Jan in the play?

   Write about:

   - some of the ways that Kelly presents the characters of Mark and Jan.
   - the way Kelly uses the characters of Mark and Jan to present some of his ideas.

5. 'Despite being mostly absent, it is Adam who is the central character of *DNA*.' How far do you agree with this statement?

   Write about:

   - some of the ways that Kelly presents the character of Adam
   - the way Kelly uses the character of Adam to present some of his ideas.

6. How does Kelly present Brian in *DNA*?

   Write about:

   - some of the ways that Kelly presents the character of Brian
   - the way Kelly uses the character of Brian to present some of his ideas.

7. Who do you think is the most powerful character in *DNA*?

   Write about:

   - how different characters behave in ways that make them seem powerful
   - how Kelly presents some characters as being more powerful than others.

8. 'Cathy is the most changed character by the end of the play.' How does Kelly present the character of Cathy?

   Write about:

   - the ways that Cathy changes through the play
   - the way that Kelly presents Cathy in the ways that he writes.

9. 'DNA presents a completely negative view of human nature.' How far do you agree with this statement?

Write about:

- some of Kelly's ideas about human nature
- the way Kelly presents these ideas by the ways he writes.

10. John Tate: 'Haven't I been trying to keep everyone together?'

Explore the way that Kelly presents ideas about community in the play.

Write about:

- how Kelly uses his characters to explore ideas about community
- how Kelly presents community in the ways that he writes.

11. Explore the way that Kelly presents ideas about responsibility in the play.

Write about:

- how Kelly uses his characters to explore ideas about responsibility
- how Kelly presents responsibility in the ways that he writes.

12. Explore the way that Kelly presents ideas about violence in the play.

Write about:

- some of the violent events in the play
- how Kelly presents violence by the ways that he writes.

13. 'Kelly does not present teenagers as evil – they are ordinary people caught up in events they can't control.' How does Kelly present teenagers in the play?

Write about:

- some of the ideas Kelly explores about being a teenager
- the way Kelly presents these ideas by the ways that he writes.

14. How effective is the ending of *DNA*?

Write about:

- how the ending of the play presents important ideas
- how Kelly presents these ideas by the ways that he writes.

15. How does Kelly present different attitudes towards society in *DNA*?

Write about:

- what different characters' attitudes are to society
- how Kelly presents attitudes to society by the ways that he writes.

16. How does Kelly present ideas about bullies and victims in *DNA*?

Write about:

- what some of the ideas about bullies and victims are
- the way Kelly presents these ideas by the ways that he writes.

Planning a Character Question Response

You must be able to: understand what an exam question is asking you and prepare your response.

How might an exam question on character be phrased?

A typical character question will read like this:

How far does Kelly present Leah as a moral character?

Write about:

- some of the ways that Kelly presents the character of Leah
- the way Kelly uses the character of Leah to present some of his ideas.

[30 marks + 4 AO4 marks]

How do I work out what to do?

The focus of this question is on Leah and how far she is a moral character. The bullet points remind you that you should discuss who Leah is, her role in the play, and the language, structure and form that Kelly uses to create her.

For AO1, you need to show a critical response, which means exploring how Leah can be considered moral, and any ways in which she is not.

For AO2, you need to analyse the ways Kelly uses language, structure and form to show what Leah is like and suggest her morality, or lack of it. You should include analysing Kelly's techniques in the whole play.

For AO3, you need to link your comments to the play's historical, social and literary contexts and write accurately to pick up your four AO4 marks for spelling, punctuation and grammar.

How do I plan my essay?

You have approximately 45 minutes to write your essay.

Although it doesn't seem long, spending the first five minutes writing a quick plan helps to focus your thoughts and produce a well-structured essay, an essential part of AO1.

Try to think of five or six ideas. Each of these can become a paragraph.

You can plan however you find most useful – a list, spider-diagram or flow chart. Once you have your ideas, take a moment to check which order you want to write them in. Look at the example on the opposite page.

Is Leah a moral character?

Leah's moral actions:

- wanting to take Adam back
- 'But he's not dead. He's alive' / known him since children's birthday parties.
- engaging with moral and philosophical issues ('Happy is our natural and any deviation from that state is seen as a failure')
- change from monologues, to silence at the end *'gets up, stares at Phil. Storms off.'*

Leah's immoral actions:

- killing her hamster – 'I put the point of a screwdriver on his head and I hit it with a hammer'

Relationships with others:

- she's closest to Phil but doesn't seem to know him well – surprised by his actions
- logical and rational; caring towards Adam (speaks 'kindly')

Summary

- Make sure you know what the focus of the essay is.
- Remember to analyse how ideas are conveyed by Kelly.
- Try to relate your ideas to the play's social and historical context.

Questions

QUICK TEST
1. What key skills do you need to show in your answer?
2. What are the benefits of quickly planning your essay?
3. Why is it better to have learned quotations for the exam?

EXAM PRACTICE
Plan a response to Question 2 on page 60.
How far does Kelly present Phil as being in control through the play?
Write about:
- some of the ways that Phil is in control
- the way Kelly presents these ideas by the ways he writes.
[30 marks + 4 AO4 marks]

Grade 5 Annotated Response

How far does Kelly present Leah as a moral character?

Write about:

- some of the ways that Kelly presents the character of Leah
- the way Kelly uses the character of Leah to present some of his ideas.

[30 marks + 4 AO4 marks]

Kelly presents Leah as one of the more moral characters in the play because she protests about killing Adam and seems shocked by some of the violence. (1) However, she also has some immoral actions, which shows that everyone has violence inside them. (2)

It seems like Leah and Phil weren't directly involved in Adam's death as John Tate says 'You're clever. So what do we do?' This question (3) shows that the gang look up to Leah and Phil, so Leah could be seen as a moral compass guiding them all. They must be told what has happened. This suggests that although she might have been part of the bullying she wasn't part of Adam's death. Phil doesn't give her anything to do in the cover-up. She is silent although she is onstage, (4) so her only immoral action is not saying anything. Dennis Kelly is writing about children being isolated from society without institutions like the police or schools being influential in their lives, (5) so it makes sense Leah wouldn't betray her friends. Leah might be seen as doing the moral thing by not saying anything as that would ruin everyone else's lives. (6)

Leah has lots of monologues in the play representing its themes. She talks about the small differences in DNA between bonobos and chimpanzees which could mean that people also behave in different ways because of how they are made, which explains different responses to Adam when he returns. Leah is naive about Phil's plan and this shows her moral centre because she doesn't even think about killing Adam. She says 'we can explain, we can talk. We can go through the whole thing'. She uses the plural pronoun 'we' showing she believes they are still a unit although Phil and Cathy have decided something without her. She also worries if Adam comes back 'next week, next year,' using the time phrases to show that there is a possibility of this happening in the future and her morality means that she doesn't realise what Phil is planning. She tells Phil 'But he's not dead. He's alive'. These simple utterances with the blunt contrast of 'dead' and 'alive' (7) show that she is naive and unable to see that Phil already thinks of Adam as dead. She also reminds Phil that they knew Adam as a child 'he used to have that cheap ice cream and we used to take the piss, remember?', which tries to make Phil feel empathy and a relationship with Adam, to make him treat him in a moral way. In contrast to Leah, Cathy and Phil decide to kill Adam. Phil putting a bag over Brian's head is a shocking visual, especially as Brian doesn't understand what's happening and sees it as a game. The secretive locations, like the wood, make it difficult for Leah to win the argument as Kelly uses this setting to show that the teenagers are isolated from society, trying to work out for themselves what is moral and what isn't. (8)

However, Leah is also sometimes violent, which can be shocking for an audience. (9) She shows Phil a box with her hamster in it: 'I put the point of a screwdriver on his head and I hit it with a hammer'. This blunt matter-of-fact tone demonstrates the pointlessness of her violence, almost as though she is just experimenting to see what would happen. She might also mime the action onstage, which would be even more disturbing. (10) Kelly is exploring what happens when children are isolated from society and suggesting that they become violent because the rules don't apply to them, which shows that humans are all immoral unless controlled by society.

By the end, Leah leaves the gang, showing there can be moral redemption. (11) She is upset with Phil and 'spits the sweet out'. This stage direction shows her unhappiness and anger with Phil. When she changes schools, she is showing moral strength because she decides to leave everyone behind, but it is also ambiguous because she still hasn't said anything about the real murder. (12)

1. Clear opening argument linked with the question. AO1
2. Links character with key theme. AO1
3. Explanation of quotation with subject vocabulary, could be more embedded. AO2
4. Considering what the play looks like onstage. AO2
5. Referring to literary context of the writer's intention. Could be more integrated into the main paragraph. AO3
6. Comes back to the language of the question regularly. AO1
7. Using subject vocabulary and explaining writer's methods. AO2
8. Applying context to the theme. AO3
9. Considers alternative viewpoints. AO1
10. Interpretation of stagecraft/form. AO2
11. Show good knowledge of the whole play. AO1
12. Conclusion summarises the main response to the question. Response is well written with accuracy and control. AO4

Questions

EXAM PRACTICE
Choose a paragraph of this essay, read it through a few times, then try to improve it. You might:
- replace a reference with a quotation
- analyse a quotation in more depth, including terminology
- improve the range of analysis of methods
- improve the expression, or sophistication of the vocabulary
- connect more context to the analysis.

Grade 7+ Annotated Response

How far does Kelly present Leah as a moral character?

Write about:

- some of the ways that Kelly presents the character of Leah
- the way Kelly uses the character of Leah to present some of his ideas.

[30 marks + 4 AO4 marks]

Kelly presents Leah as a relatively moral character – however, even her morality is dubious. She is occasionally violent and doesn't confess Adam's death to the authorities. Through Leah, Kelly questions what actions could be moral if they are done to protect people. (1)

Leah is part of the ongoing bullying as she 'took the piss out of him', with the colloquialism minimising the distress this caused. However, she isn't directly involved in his death as she is told about it. John Tate calls on her, saying 'You're clever. So what do we do?' The question and adjective position Leah as more knowledgeable or moral, guiding their actions. (2) Her immorality is staying silent. (3)

Kelly uses settings to explore the impact of alienation on Leah's morality; scenes take place in secluded places like the wood where the ensemble meets. This symbolises the lack of involvement with social institutions like the police or schools, and the lack of support that teenagers often feel they get from society. (4) When characters like Danny are concerned about their future ('A levels are the plan. Dead people aren't the plan.') it makes sense Leah wouldn't betray her friends as social institutions would condemn, rather than help, them. Kelly explores how far it's moral to sacrifice the individual for the many: Leah's silence protects the future of her friends – Adam can't be brought back from the dead. (5)

Through Leah, Kelly asks the audience to question their responses to Adam's two deaths. Her Act 3 monologue draws attention to the construction of the play: 'a lot bigger than all this, these people, sitting here … exit stage left Leah, right now.' (6) The language of theatre ('stage left') and direct reference to the audience ('these people') break the fourth wall as Kelly asks the audience to question who the moral characters are. Leah's monologues have a similar function as they are different to the clipped, fast-paced dialogue in the rest of the play. They are often long, contrasted with Phil's silence onstage beside her, and they cast light on key themes. For example, she says bonobos are 'exactly like chimps, but the tiniest change in their DNA' changes them from vicious, preying on the weak, to empathetic and kind. This echoes through the play up to Adam's reappearance. (7) Phil and Cathy are symbolically the chimps; they decide to kill Adam with shocking violence. Phil puts a plastic bag on Brian, who in his vulnerability sees it as a game, but onstage visuals convey Phil's intention to the audience. Leah's basic morality here makes her naive. (8) She says, 'we can explain … We can go through the whole thing.' The plural pronoun indicates she still believes they are deciding as a unit, although it is clear through the staging that Phil and Cathy have decided without her.

Kelly shows Leah's morality through her struggles to come to terms with what has happened. In Act 2 she becomes sarcastic towards Phil, as even though 'everyone's happy', after Adam's death, she comments 'you know, omelettes and eggs, as long as you've your waffle, who cares.' This black humour, with the **idiom** *and dismissive subordinate clause, might make an audience laugh but reflects Kelly's theme of sacrifice of the individual for the many. (9) By the end Leah leaves the gang, which represents some moral redemption, although it's ambiguous as she hasn't confessed Adam's murder to anybody.*

Elsewhere, there is further ambiguity. (10) She shows her hamster to Phil: 'I put the point of a screwdriver on his head and I hit it with a hammer.' The blunt, cold tone implies that violence is inherent in everybody, particularly when children are isolated from external influences to guide their morality – which in turn suggests people don't have an innate understanding of right and wrong but must learn it through example and experience, and that it isn't black and white. (11)

Leah is perhaps the most moral character but isn't completely moral as her silence makes her culpable for Adam's final death – a way for Kelly to warn that not speaking out is just as tragic and immoral. (12)

1. Links character with themes and addresses the question. AO1
2. Confident analysis with subject terminology. AO2
3. Consideration of stagecraft. AO2
4. Link to social and literary context. AO3
5. Mini-conclusion to a paragraph, including link to applied context. AO3
6. Confident topic sentence focusing on writer's methods. AO2/AO3
7. Confident references to the whole play. AO1
8. Regular reference to question. AO1
9. Detailed analysis with subject terminology. AO2
10. Consideration of alternative interpretations. AO1
11. Applied context linked to writer's meaning. AO1/AO3
12. Confident conclusion. Essay is written accurately with precise vocabulary. AO1/AO4

Questions

EXAM PRACTICE
Spend 45 minutes writing an answer to Question 2 on page 60.
How far does Kelly present Phil as being in control through the play?
Write about:
- some of the ways that Phil is in control
- the way Kelly presents these ideas by the ways he writes.
[30 marks + 4 AO4 marks]
Remember to use the plan you have already prepared.

Planning a Theme Question Response

You must be able to: understand what an exam question is asking you and prepare your response.

How might an exam question on theme be phrased?

A typical theme question will read like this:

'*DNA* presents a completely negative view of human nature.' How far do you agree with this statement?

Write about:

- some of Kelly's ideas about human nature
- the way Kelly presents these ideas by the ways he writes.

[30 marks + 4 AO4 marks]

How do I work out what to do?

The focus of this play is on human nature and Kelly's ideas, meaning whether humans are innately good or evil. There is a quotation, which you can use to strengthen your argument (e.g. if it is completely negative or there are some positive aspects). Sometimes, there will be a quotation from a character which you can use in the same way.

The bullet points remind you that you should discuss what Kelly's ideas about human nature are, and the language, structure and form that Kelly uses to present these ideas.

For AO1, you need to show a critical response, which means exploring what human nature is like in the play, and how negative it is.

For AO2, you need to analyse the ways Kelly uses language, structure and form to show different interpretations about human nature. You should include analysing Kelly's techniques in the whole play.

For AO3, you need to link your comments to the play's historical, social and literary contexts and write accurately to pick up your four AO4 marks for spelling, punctuation and grammar.

How do I plan my essay?

You have approximately 45 minutes to write your essay.

Although it doesn't seem long, spending the first five minutes writing a quick plan helps to focus your thoughts and produce a well-structured essay, an essential part of AO1.

Try to think of five or six ideas. Each of these can become a paragraph.

You can plan however you find most useful – a list, spider-diagram or flow chart. Once you have your ideas, take a moment to check which order you want to write them in. Look at the example on the opposite page.

***DNA* might be seen as presenting a completely negative view of human nature**

The characters behave immorally and don't take responsibility for their actions:

- torturing Adam – laughing about it
- LEAH: [Chimps] kill and sometimes torture each other to find a better position within the social structure. (2.3)
- AO3 – gangs, power

Characters become more cruel through the play:

- Cathy's transition to 'running things'
- Phil – progressing from manslaughter to murder – 'You'll drop through. You'll fall into the cold. Into the dark. You'll land on Adam's corpse and you'll rot together.' (2.3)
- AO3 – individual vs many

However, Kelly presents some positive aspects of human nature:

- some are kinder after Adam's first death

Impact on characters indicates their morality, and whether their natures are good:

- characters who leave (Leah 'suddenly she stops chewing and spits the sweet out ... storms off', 4.2)
- Brian's descent to madness – 'I'm crying because I'm lying and I feel terrible inside' (2.3)

Summary

- Make sure you know what the focus of the essay is.
- Remember to analyse how ideas are conveyed by Kelly.
- Try to relate your ideas to the play's social and historical context.

Questions

QUICK TEST
1. What key skills do you need to show in your answer?
2. What are the benefits of quickly planning your essay?
3. Why is it better to have learned quotations for the exam?

EXAM PRACTICE
Plan a response to Question 10 on page 61.
John Tate: 'Haven't I been trying to keep everyone together?'
Explore the way that Kelly presents ideas about community in the play.
Write about:
- how Kelly uses his characters to explore ideas about community
- how Kelly presents community in the ways that he writes.
[30 marks + 4 AO4 marks]

Grade 5 Annotated Response

'*DNA* presents a completely negative view of human nature.' How far do you agree with this statement?

Write about:

- some of Kelly's ideas about human nature
- the way Kelly presents these ideas by the ways he writes.

[30 marks + 4 AO4 marks]

Kelly shows that human nature is mostly negative as his characters get increasingly violent and do cruel things including killing Adam deliberately. (1)

Kelly shows that his characters are bullies from the beginning, although they don't take responsibility for their actions. Mark says: 'we were having a laugh, weren't we.' This rhetorical statement shows he has doubts about it and is justifying himself. They were stubbing out cigarettes and making him eat leaves, but they weren't trying to kill him so they aren't evil (2) although their natures have some evil in them. Leah's monologue is a metaphor (3) of chimps showing that the characters in the play are like chimps, because they behave cruelly and bully individuals if it means the group is better off. An audience might think they should be more like bonobos, who have empathy. They would also think this because Kelly uses settings that could be anywhere, because they are generic like 'a street, a field and a wood,' meaning that events could happen regardless of location.

Kelly explains human nature can change, and people can become crueller, like Cathy. (4) At the start, she's having fun causing arguments but she has no empathy and describes Adam's death as 'exciting' which is a callous adjective showing her coldness. At the end, she murders Adam and is 'running things', showing her importance and how she's taken control through violence. This is like the chimps using violence to control the group. 'She cut a first year's finger off. That's what they say, anyway.' (5) Contextually, Kelly uses ideas about how teenagers are seen by society and dehumanised like they are evil. (6)

Phil also gets more violent, which is a negative side of human nature. He uses a semantic field of death to threaten Brian. 'You'll fall into the cold. Into the dark. You'll land on Adam's corpse and you'll rot together.' This imagery is vicious and gruesome. The short sentences make it more frightening because it's describing what will happen not what might happen. This shows an audience how Phil has a dark side to his nature. (7) Phil thinks he is protecting everyone and uses a rhetorical question: 'What's more important, one person or everyone?' He has decided to kill Adam and wants Leah to agree. This is an example of Kelly speaking to the audience through a character as it makes an audience think about their response. They might have sympathy for characters whose futures would be affected if Adam comes back, and the cover-up and bullying are discovered, but they might also think that murder is always wrong. (8)

There are some good sides of people as well as negative human natures. (9) Brian feels guilty, as Richard says, 'they're going to section him', which is a sad end. Most characters aren't involved in the murder and try to do something good after the cover-up. Richard is friendlier and Mark does charity work. This shows they feel guilty, so their human natures can't be evil. The cover-up could be because they're frightened, like Danny saying he needs 'references'. They are just trying to protect themselves.

Leah also shows good in human nature. She can be violent, and kills her hamster, but then tries to convince Phil to let Adam come back. In the last act 'suddenly she stops chewing and spits the sweet out ... storms off.' Spitting the sweet out symbolises her rejecting Phil, like she's rejecting him through the food he's given her. Leaving the group shows that she's trying to make a better life for herself. (10)

Kelly shows that human nature can be good or evil but it depends on interpretations. He asks the audience whether there are definite boundaries, or if we are all a bit of both. Although some of his characters might sometimes do good things he has quite a negative view. (11)

1. Short introduction focused on key term. AO1

2. Specific references. AO1

3. Use of subject terminology. Could analyse the language more. AO2

4. Clear focus on the question. AO1

5. Useful quotation, could be embedded. AO1

6. Reference to relevant context. Could be more applied. AO3

7. Interpretation of language with subject terminology. AO2

8. Focus on the audience response. AO2

9. Exploration of the question. AO1

10. Using characters to connect to the theme. AO2

11. Clear conclusion summarising the ideas. Spelling, punctuation and grammar are consistently accurate. AO1/AO4

Questions

EXAM PRACTICE
Choose a paragraph of this essay, read it through a few times, then try to improve it. You might:

- replace a reference with a quotation
- analyse a quotation in more depth, including terminology
- improve the range of analysis of methods
- improve the expression, or sophistication of the vocabulary
- connect more context to the analysis.

Grade 7+ Annotated Response

'*DNA* presents a completely negative view of human nature.' How far do you agree with this statement?

Write about:

- some of Kelly's ideas about human nature
- the way Kelly presents these ideas by the ways he writes.

[30 marks + 4 AO4 marks]

Kelly's characters behave in immoral or amoral ways, primarily their violence and cruelty towards Adam, which is compounded by his deliberate murder. Yet Kelly explores whether this is simply part of human nature trying to protect themselves and their group – and whether sacrificing the individual for the community is right. (1)

Kelly establishes their immoral behaviour in the description of the bullying as Mark and Jan's stichomythia (Jan: Stubbed out cigarettes on him/Mark: joking, we were) juxtaposes their brutal violence with humour. However, it's clear through the repetition of 'laugh' and 'joking' (2) that they are trying to justify their actions and explain things went too far. Adam's death is also clearly accidental, implying their human natures aren't evil. In fact, Kelly rejects the idea of good and evil. In Leah's monologue he uses the metaphor of bonobos and chimps who 'kill and sometimes torture each other to find a better position within the social structure.' This matter-of-fact tone, with scientific information, suggests the teenagers are more like chimps and are driven by animalistic impulses. However, the contrasting empathy of the bonobos implies that Kelly believes humans have both good and evil in them and must choose which to be. (3)

Several characters become crueller through the play, suggesting that they are more confident in behaving as their natures dictate. (4) Cathy's initially a troublemaker, saying Danny is 'on Richard's side' to cause friction. She uses the callous adjective 'exciting' to describe Adam's death, demonstrating her lack of empathy. Kelly shows how she changes and becomes progressively crueller; first, deliberately framing an innocent man, then leading Adam to his death. This echoes the chimps in Leah's monologue as it enhances her social position: she is 'running things' and 'has cut a first year's finger off,' with rumours of violence and cruelty also consolidating her position through fear.

Phil also demonstrates the violence of human nature when he threatens Brian. The imagery of 'cold', 'dark' and 'Adam's corpse ... you'll rot together' emphasises the brutality of his threat. Yet Phil doesn't see himself as evil, but rather as protecting the group. He asks Leah 'Everyone is happier. What's more important, one person or everyone?' Repetition of 'everyone', and his rhetorical question, suggest he sees himself protecting everyone around him. (5) Problematically, he is right; their aspirations would be ruined if Adam reappears. Kelly asks how far it's worth privileging an individual's life as the positive outcomes of Adam's death on the wider community seem to outweigh the negatives. Kelly's use of dramatic techniques, including his non-gender-specific characters and generic settings of 'a street, a field and a wood', make his play representative of all communities. Audiences can maintain emotional detachment and question whether sacrificing Adam's life is worth it. (6) However, audiences also bring their cultural belief that murder is wrong and remember the metaphor of the chimps sacrificing the weak to protect others, which would make them question whether human nature should be more noble.

Kelly also presents some positive aspects of human nature, although with dark consequences. Brian is destroyed, describing 'crying because I'm lying and I feel terrible inside', with the guilt consequently driving him towards a breakdown. Leah, too, demonstrates more positive humanity as Cathy's opposite, transitioning from leader (asked for advice) to being unable to persuade Phil to listen to her. Kelly associates her more with violence earlier, killing her hamster 'with a screwdriver'. Eventually she becomes a more moral character, abandoning Phil. The stage directions say 'suddenly she stops chewing and spits the sweet out ... storms off'. Spitting the sweet out is a final physical, visual rejection of Phil's actions, and it's the last time she's onstage before completely separating herself. (7) Even Leah, however, doesn't do the ultimate moral thing and confess to the authorities.

Kelly doesn't make a decisive argument for human nature being positive or negative, but explores how far people will go to protect themselves and their communities. He warns that when threatened, people are capable of doing terrible things as long as they feel they can justify them. (8)

1. A confident opening giving a response to the question. AO1

2. Analysis of language with subject vocabulary. AO2

3. Applied use of context. AO3

4. Analysis of structure, for example, character development. AO2

5. Developed analysis of language with subject vocabulary. AO2

6. Embedding context to explain specific choices of language and narrative. AO3

7. Analysis of stagecraft and visuals. AO2

8. Thoughtful conclusion with final interpretation. Spelling, punctuation and grammar are accurate and sophisticated throughout. AO1/AO4

Questions

EXAM PRACTICE
Spend 45 minutes writing an answer to Question 10 on page 61.
John Tate: 'Haven't I been trying to keep everyone together?'
Explore the way that Kelly presents ideas about community in the play. Write about:
• how Kelly uses his characters to explore ideas about community
• how Kelly presents community in the ways that he writes.
[30 marks + 4 AO4 marks]
Remember to use the plan you have already prepared.

Glossary

Act – a section of a play, divided into scenes.

Adjective – a word that describes a noun.

Aggravate – make a problem worse.

Antagonistic – showing active opposition or hostility.

Aspirational – wanting to achieve social or material success.

Atmosphere – a tone, mood or general feeling.

Binary opposition – two related concepts opposite in meaning.

Black comedy – a comic style making light of dark or taboo subjects.

Callous – uncaring and cruel.

Cathartic – providing psychological relief by expressing strong emotion.

Characteristics – typical qualities of a character.

Chorus – in Greek drama, a group of performers who comment on the main action.

Clause – a group of words that includes a main verb and could stand as a sentence.

Claustrophobia – fear of being in confined enclosed space.

Cliché – an overused phrase which lacks original thought.

Colloquialism – everyday, slang word.

Connotation – an underlying or deeper meaning suggested by a word.

Cyclical (structure) – repeating in cycles, the end returning to the beginning.

Dehumanise – reduce from human.

Determiner – a word that shows whether a reference is specific (such as: this, that, your, his) or general (such as: a, an, any).

Discourse marker – a word that organises thoughts (such as: so, well, next, firstly).

Duologue – a section of a play with only two speaking roles.

Dynamics – the relationships and emotions between the characters.

Echo – refer to a previous event or similar scene or idea.

Elevated – highly poetic or romanticised speech.

Empathy – the ability to share and understand the feelings of another person.

Enigma – something that is mysterious, difficult to understand.

Ensemble – a group of actors performing together.

Exposition – the opening part of a play where setting and characters are introduced.

Euphemism – a mild way of saying something too harsh or unpleasant to refer to.

Foreshadow – hint at future events in the play.

Fourth wall – the space separating a performer from the audience.

Fragmented sentences – very short groups of words that look like sentences but aren't grammatically complete (such as: 'oh no'/'of us').

Garrulous – excessively talkative, especially on trivial matters.

Idiom – a common saying or phrase.

Imagery – words used to create a picture in the imagination.

Implicit – not directly expressed.

In media res – in the middle of things; a narrative opening in the midst of action.

Irony – something that seems the opposite of what was expected; the deliberate use of words that mean the opposite of what is intended.

Juxtapose – to place two contrasting things side by side.

Machiavelli – Italian diplomat and writer (b. 1469, d. 1527), known for recommending deceitful and unscrupulous behaviour in politics.

Manipulative – influencing or coercing another person or situation.

Melodrama – exaggerated drama.

Metaphor – a descriptive technique, using comparison to say one thing is something else.

Meta-theatre – aspects of a play that call attention to its fictional nature as drama or theatre.

Monologue – a long speech by a single actor.

Moral panic – public anxiety in response to a problem concerning the potential decline of society's morals.

Naive – showing a lack of experience, wisdom or judgement.

Narrator – the person telling the story or delivering a commentary alongside the action.

Naturalistic – representing something as if it were natural.

Offstage – not seen by the audience.

Pace – the comparative speed of events or dialogue.

Parallelism – repetitive grammatical structures used one after the other.

Pathos – writing or situation that causes feelings of pity or sorrow.

Pause – a temporary stop in action or speech.

Philosophise – study the nature of knowledge, reality and existence.

Precipitate – to cause an event or situation, often suddenly or unexpectedly.

Primitive – referring to society at an early stage in historical social development.

Psychological – affecting a person's mental or emotional state.

Representational – in theatre, to create an impression or idea of the costume, staging or set without using naturalistic detail.

Rhetorical (question) – a statement made (or a question asked) for effect, without expecting a response.

Rituals – a series of actions in a prescribed order.

Sarcastic – using irony to mock or convey contempt.

Sectioned – kept and treated in hospital because of mental health problems, possibly without the individual's agreement.

Semantic – related to meaning.

Setting – the visual location of a play.

Simile – a descriptive technique, using comparison to say one thing is 'like' or 'as' something else.

Slang – language using informal words and phrases.

Social institution – a group constructed to fulfil a common purpose of society (such as: law and order, educational, religious).

Stage directions – instructions in a script indicating movement, position or tone of an actor, or staging including sound, lighting and scenery.

Stichomythia – lines in a play alternating between two characters but repeating certain words to emphasise specific ideas.

Structure – organisation of a phrase, scene, act or whole text.

Subvert – to undermine expectations in a deliberate way, often to make a point about their inaccuracy or unfairness.

Symbolise – to use an object or colour to represent a specific idea or meaning.

Syndetic – repeated use of conjunctions.

Tone – the quality, emotion or mood of writing or speech.

Triadic structure – repeating three similar words/phrases for emphasis.

Utterance – a spoken word or statement.

Verb – a doing, feeling, thinking or being word.

Victim – a person harmed, injured or killed because of a crime or accident or others' behaviour.

Visceral – affecting deep inner feelings, often in a grotesque or disturbing way.

Answers

Analysis could include: Leah's repetition of positive vocabulary, the short clauses suggesting she is sarcastic; the simile of Adam's fear, suggestive of comfort rather than coming back to face the outside world that destroyed him, creating pathos in the juxtaposition of the two situations; or the stage direction's description creating a visual impression of the gulf between Adam and the others in the noun 'aliens' and his uncomfortable 'twitching.'

Pages 4–5

Quick Test

1. He was tormented, bullied, and harmed, then walked over a grille while others threw stones at him. He fell in, and they believe he's dead.
2. To create a false trail of evidence that suggests someone has kidnapped Adam.
3. At first, John Tate, although there is some leadership conflict with Richard. Phil takes charge.
4. They are empathetic and kind, unlike chimpanzees, who attack the weak and outsiders. This symbolises two opposing types of human behaviour.

Exam Practice

Answers could include the humour in Mark and Jan's duologue. Analysis could also include Leah's near-hysterical list of fast-paced clauses and the apparent insecurity she expresses in her monologue, projecting her own thoughts towards Phil, and the shockingly violent suggestion to 'rip out my teeth', or her metaphor of DNA referencing human nature.

Pages 6–7

Quick Test

1. The police have found someone who matches the fictional description, whose DNA was on the jumper that Cathy, Mark and Danny stole.
2. Because Cathy and Mark took the jumper to the sorting office and found someone who matched the invented description.
3. Kelly is suggesting that there is no 'order' in humanity. Leah implies that the pressure to be 'happy' makes life feel more miserable, and that chaos is the natural state for people to be in.
4. She keeps reminding people that they made the 'killer' up – she is horrified by Cathy and Mark's actions.
5. When Brian refuses to identify the man in custody, Phil threatens to kill him in the same way that Adam died.

Exam Practice

Answers could include the unexpected violence from Leah, and the blunt simple vocabulary she utters to describe the death of her pet. Analysis could consider the change in Cathy's character including her hesitant 'you know', suggesting doubt in her changing role. However, she also says she is miserable. Could also explore the way events are getting out of their control in framing someone in the confusion of Leah/Lou's dialogue.

Pages 8–9

Quick Test

1. She says she wants to run away, to get a reaction from Phil, but it doesn't work.
2. Leah says people are happier, as though they value their own lives more. However, she also says she is miserable, and that Brian and John Tate are having difficult times.
3. He found his way out, badly injured, and has been living in a hedge foraging but unable to get home.
4. Phil puts a plastic bag over Brian's head, demonstrating to Cathy how she should kill Adam.
5. Phil doesn't listen when she tries to persuade him they can go to the authorities to explain what happened to Adam. In the field, she doesn't speak but first takes and then rejects his offer of food and storms off crying.

Pages 10–11

Quick Test

1. Brian has a breakdown; Danny sees people's mouths as holes like the one Adam fell into; John Tate has found god; Cathy and Lou are running things; Mark and Jan are shoplifting; Leah has moved schools; Phil isn't eating; Richard has replaced Leah's role in the field with Phil, asking him to come back and lead the group.
2. It has two scenes, not four. It is missing a group scene, and has only one scene in the field, with Richard and not Leah with Phil.
3. The lack of unity in the group – everything has fallen apart.
4. Richard, not Leah.

Exam Practice

Answers might include the summary of each character's life now, the different paths they've taken (violence or trauma), and the similar, but broken, structure of Act 4 compared with the others. Analysis might include: the simile of falling into mouths reminiscent of Adam's death; Richard's monologue with the alien imagery suggesting how distant from society they have all become, or the qualifier 'anyway' suggesting a lack of belief.

Pages 12–13

Quick Test

1. The short timescale, with gaps between acts but no interval, creates a fast pace as the events unfold rapidly, outside the characters' control.
2. It implies that events are unchangeable, that they will continue to happen in a cycle, and cannot be stopped.
3. There are two scenes, not four – the group scenes are missing, showing the destruction of the group. It could suggest escape, but not to a better situation.
4. Replacing Leah with Richard implies that not much has changed for Phil. His silence could show he is affected by events, or that he continues to be uninterested.

Exam Practice

Answers could explore the settings as being public but lonely, outside the usual social spaces and deserted except for the play's characters. Analysis could also consider the repetitive cycle to create an almost claustrophobic sense that the characters are trapped, inside society, and forced to turn to one another. Analysis could also use the stage direction of 'silence' to explore the lack of communication throughout the play and the pause this creates onstage for the audience to consider their response to events.

Pages 14–15

Quick Test

1. Very little. They go to school and meet the police, but all this occurs offstage and in a distanced way, as though the institutions have little influence.
2. They associated them with anti-social, violent or criminal behaviour, and involvement with sex and alcohol .
3. To change the dynamic of the relationships (a dramatic choice).
4. She wants to be famous.

Exam Practice

Answers could explore Kelly's presentation of teens as needlessly violent, disaffected, uninvolved with social institutions and their boundaries, or seeking celebrity via the media. Responses could also look at the way that the play's characters are callous, careless and violent, reflecting the often negative, even dehumanised, view of teens in the media. Analysis could include the despair evident in Danny's need to obtain three references.

Pages 16–17

Quick Test

1. They allow production teams to stage the play in their own way. They remind the audience of the construction of the play.
2. It questions assumptions based on gender – who is more likely to lead, bully or be cruel.
3. Both create silences. Pauses are slightly longer. Beats suggest a change in character or relationship.
4. It uses shocking and controversial subjects enabling Kelly to explore contemporary young people's lives.
5. By using minimalistic set, props and costume, keeping the production representational so the audience think about his themes rather than seeking catharsis.

Exam Practice

Answers might include: the minimal stage directions and Leah's monologue drawing attention to the play as a constructed piece designed to provoke thought; the use of gender to influence or challenge the audience's response to themes, for example, leadership, morality and cruelty; the stage directions being open to interpretation to keep the production relevant to the community in which it is staged.

Pages 18–19

Quick Test

1. A street, a field and a wood.
2. The street is a public space but is empty except for Mark and Jan; the field is open but secluded from society; the wood is private, secretive and hidden from society. The characters move from the more public to the hidden in each act.
3. Jan and Mark's conversations in the street would be impossible for a passerby to decipher; the field could be interpreted as a potentially romantic setting for Phil and Leah, but their relationship is ambiguous; the wood provides a secret meeting place for the group, highlighting their alienation from society.
4. DNA is used to explain the difference between chimps and bonobos, and represents different ways for humans to behave towards one another. DNA is considered to be unquestionable evidence but is manipulated in the play, linking to themes of deception and violence.

Exam Practice

Answers could include: the enigma caused by duologues in the street where mysterious conversations may be overheard; the use of the wood and field as secretive places outside adult control where teenagers control their own lives.

Pages 20–21

Quick Test

1. They begin each act in a public street. Their repeated phrases create mystery, which is explained in the scene in the secretive space (the wood). They also narrate offstage action, such as Adam's death and Leah's departure.
2. They are both involved in Adam's death and the bullying that preceded it. Mark, with Cathy, is also partly responsible for framing the innocent postman. Neither seem to fully accept responsibility, and are concerned they will get into trouble.
3. They use short repetitive utterances to reassure each other or to justify themselves. They also create mystery, through their lack of specificity in the street scenes. Their slang contrasts the lightness of their language with the violence they are describing.

Exam Practice

Answers could include the characters' roles as narrators, guiding the audience in the action and describing the offstage actions. Analysis could include the repetition and short utterances, and the pace/tone of these duologues creating a light-hearted or comic feel at odds with the violence of the events. Their duologues demonstrate their heartlessness and lack of empathy for Adam and reveal their main concern is about getting into trouble.

Pages 22–23

Quick Test

1. He takes control from John Tate when Adam's 'death' is revealed. He dominates the cover-up.
   •

2. Through violence, threats and implicit commands. His silence can be controlling.
3. Initially, there may be a romantic element – it is unclear. They are always together in the field, although he doesn't speak and simply eats. She finally decides he has gone too far and leaves, after he seems to show physical affection. This might be a coercive act, considering its timing in the play.
4. It gives him an opportunity to watch others. It sometimes provides black comedy. When Leah is gone, he stops eating, which could be as a result of her disappearance from his life, or because he's affected by the events of the play.

Exam Practice

Answers might include the way he explicitly takes control of the situation and the group, or explore the issue of happiness. Analysis might include: the violent repetition and separation of 'we' and 'you' when he threatens Brian in 2.3, placing himself with the rest of the group; his persuasive argument that the group is more important than the individual; how stage directions present him as compassionate towards Lou when he is really manipulating her.

Pages 24–25

Quick Test

1. She constantly wants his attention. She is overly melodramatic and sometimes violent to herself.
2. They raise philosophical questions linked to the play's themes. They prepare an audience for her to be talkative so her silence at the end of Act 3 has more impact.
3. Take him back to town and tell the truth, because she now knows that he is alive.

Exam Practice

Answers should explore the contrasting sides of Leah – her rational logic, concern for the innocent postman and desire to take Adam home contrasted with her sudden violence (killing her hamster with a screwdriver). Analysis could look at her rhetorical questions suggesting a sense of hopelessness with the adjective 'doomed', adjectives describing positive states (happiness, reality) as being elevated and perhaps out of reach to people like her and the others, the stage direction indicating her bewilderment and anger with Phil and the physical rejection of him through rejecting the sweet and her leaving the stage.

Pages 26–27

Quick Test

1. A minor character who creates trouble to aggravate others.
2. She is in control, and has become increasingly violent to keep her leadership through fear.
3. She is told to plant DNA on Adam's jumper, with Mark. She waits outside the sorting office for someone fitting the invented description.
4. She finds it exciting, a change to the boredom of her life. She goes on television and enjoys the attention of being associated with Adam.
5. Causing trouble with comments at the beginning; being seen as knowledgeable about Adam on television; when she takes Brian to kill Adam; running things at the end.

Exam Practice

Answers might include: the gradual increase in her violence; her cruel use of a real person's DNA to plant on Adam's jumper; the way her power changes from simply causing trouble to causing real physical harm. Analysis might include the adjectives of 'exciting' or 'better' to describe the tragedy of Adam's death; the use of the euphemistic 'game' to describe the murder.

Answers

that the bullying has been going on for a long time, building pathos; the stage direction highlighting the violence done to him with the 'torn', 'matted', 'dried blood' visible signs of harm; the shocking nature of this as a turning point in the play; the fragmented 'woke' as he struggles to speak.

Pages 34–35

Quick Test

1. He challenges a little at first but becomes a follower, wanting Phil's attention. He becomes kinder to others, including Mark, after Adam's 'death'.
2. Sarcastic putdowns and complaints.
3. She follows without question, even accepting the cover-up story.
4. Short, simple utterances, which make her seem young.

Exam Practice

Answers could include their roles as followers, acknowledging small moments of challenging the leader but ultimately doing as they are told. Analysis could include: Lou's repetition of 'dead' contrasted with her acceptance of the cover-up in her definitive statement 'the man who killed Adam' (even though he doesn't exist); her willingness to leave Adam to die at the end; Richard's taboo language and lack of leadership or support; his expression of pity for Lou at the end.

Pages 36–37

Quick Test

1. Act 1 Scene 3.
2. He bans the word 'dead' – he is afraid and doesn't know what to do so asks Phil and Leah for help.
3. He tries to get everyone to confirm they are on 'his side' and threatens them with violence if they disagree with him.
4. He has distanced himself from everybody and found god.

Exam Practice

Answers might include the way John establishes themes of fear, violence and control in the play. His leadership propels the plot, including handing control to Phil to plan the cover-up. Analysis might include: the rhetorical questions trying to win agreement from others; the conflict of the pronouns 'we', 'my', 'You're' to ensure that he feels everyone is listening to him; the parallelism of 'sides' as an attempt to persuade the others to keep their loyalty to him; the description of him later – 'run', 'singing', 'trying' – suggestive of positivity, but futility.

Pages 38–39

Quick Test

1. Physical and psychological/emotional.
2. Weaker characters like Adam (physical) and Brian (psychological). Leah is also emotionally bullied.
3. It gives them a sense of power; for entertainment or through boredom.
4. She is a victim of Phil's emotional bullying but has also been a perpetrator of emotional bullying towards Adam.

Exam Practice

Answers could include the difference between physical and psychological bullying. Physical – Mark's description of Adam's torture. Psychological – the threatening language from Phil and Cathy. Analysis could examine the conditional phrasing (use of 'if') of the threats, playing on fear to bully Brian, the colloquial 'pegged' Mark uses to minimise the bullying, or the vague noun 'someone' to remove responsibility from a single individual.

Pages 40–41

Quick Test

1. It is common and casual; Leah seems to see it as impossible to understand.
2. By using second person and casual language like 'laughing' to minimise its importance.
3. The bullying of Adam that led to his accidental 'death' could be interpreted as an unintentional increase in violence but the deliberate threats and murder later in the play are examples of cruelty.
4. Cathy, because she sees Adam's death as exciting and finally deliberately murders him.

Pages 28–29

Quick Test

1. Adam – they are both victims of the others' bullying.
2. To tell the Head he was flashed in the woods, laying a false trail of evidence.
3. He suffers what seems like a nervous breakdown. Richard says at the end that Brian may be sectioned.
4. He becomes more repetitive and rambling, saying all his thoughts out loud and using childish imagery.

Exam Practice

Answers could include the changes Brian experiences as a result of being controlled by the others – the way he takes Adam's place as the one bullied, and the role he plays in the cover-up. Analysis could include: the repetitive short clauses when he is speaking to Leah, suggesting tension, hesitation and stuttering onstage; his comparatively calm and measured logical speech in 2.3 compared with his lack of logical thought later; the disturbing stage direction showing him eating dirt; the frightening stage direction demonstrating Phil's complete control over him.

Pages 30–31

Quick Test

1. He is more aspirational and focused on his future.
2. He is worried about getting into dental college (not about Adam's death). He is concerned that an innocent person has been framed.
3. He asks questions but doesn't act on his concerns.
4. He doesn't come onstage again. This could be because he's distanced himself from the group or because they don't trust him with Adam's reappearance.
5. He could have PTSD (post-traumatic stress disorder), suggested by his connecting people's mouths/cavities with the grille/hole into which Adam fell.

Exam Practice

Answers could explore Danny's lack of real challenge to the leaders – his desire to keep quiet, his constant concern for getting into dental college rather than the tragedy of Adam's death. Analysis could look at: the panicky tone of the first quotation along with the dark humour of 'the plan' and its repetition implying his desire to keep to it; the use of 'I' pronoun to separate himself from the rest of the group and reveal a personal concern over framing someone; the ironic use of 'right' to refer to the framing, rather than Adam's murder.

Pages 32–33

Quick Test

1. He is subject to constant bullying, which causes his 'death'. When he returns, he is murdered by Cathy and Brian.
2. Public grief including memorials, appeals and renaming buildings. For Cathy, this is a way to experience celebrity through association.
3. Fragmented and broken, showing he can't understand what's happened.
4. Under a hedge, eating animals, grasses, leaves.

Exam Practice

Answers should explore: the bullying of Adam, including Leah's comment on birthday parties and ice cream, implying

m Practice

swers could include ideas about the cruellest characters,
d the events where violence is used to force, threaten or
rm others. Analysis could explore the visceral language
Jan describing Adam's torture, Leah's metaphor of the
imps to show Cathy's rise to power in the group, or Brian's
escription of Cathy now loving violence.

ages 42–43

Quick Test

1. She uses scientific ideas in her monologues to cast light on the themes of the play.
2. The teenagers manipulate evidence against the 'postman'; as a result scientific methods are used accurately but reach an inaccurate conclusion about what happened.
3. Danny (wants to be a dentist) and Brian (on medication and at risk of being sectioned).
4. His death is described with imagery linked with beliefs about a Christian heaven; he could be seen as a primitive sacrifice.
5. He finds god and is trying to convert others. He might be trying to save himself, but not necessarily succeeding.

Exam Practice

Answers could explore: the use of religious symbolism related to Adam's death; the scientific understanding of evidence being manipulated; Leah's association with science and philosophical ideas. Analysis could explore Leah's panicky **triadic structure** related to evidence, or the imagery of light related to Adam.

Pages 44–45

Quick Test

1. Weak and powerless, leading through intimidation but only briefly.
2. They both lead through intimidation and coercion.
3. He has a good plan, and everyone does as he says.
4. She transitions from follower to leader, becoming increasingly confident in her violence.
5. Leah could be considered a moral leader; others turn to her at moments of crisis, but she lacks the confidence to make decisions without Phil.

Exam Practice

Answers could explore the way that Phil and John Tate are similar in their leadership styles (using fear), and the reasons why they are different (Phil is clever, John is not). Analysis could explore: Tate's rhetorical question or his language of respect; the silence that follows when Phil delivers his plan (showing surprise but also agreement); Phil's threat and rhetorical questioning.

ages 46–47

Quick Test

1. By describing the actions leading up to Adam's first 'death', and by visually presenting the method of his murder in Act 3.
2. Both are offstage and brutally violent. Also, Adam is unaware of what is happening in each. However, the second is deliberate murder whereas the first is accidental.
3. Rituals to help move on, for example, appeals, memorials, services – a public face of grief. People becoming happier, thinking about their lives more. She is also sarcastic about people hypocritically exaggerating grief to make themselves feel more important.

Exam Practice

Answers might include: the rituals people go through to get over death; Adam's confusion resulting from his head injury; Phil's callousness over murdering Adam because people think he's already dead, and the contrast with Leah who understands the difference. Analysis might include: Phil's list of ritualistic grief as a process to be got through; Adam's use of light imagery and its heavenly connotations; Phil's callous question and Leah's response using short utterances to show her disbelief of Phil's new plan.

ages 48–49

Quick Test

1. Feeling isolated from society.
2. As something to punish them, or something to be manipulated, not supportive. They have little impact on the characters' lives.

3. They are isolated, outside society's boundaries. Even the street (a public place) is empty – they are alone there.
4. Several scenes have small groups or pairs separate from the main group.
5. They shift allegiances through the play until they are all separated (as a group) at the end.

Exam Practice

Answers could include the different pairings through the play, the settings and structure as well as the characters' responses to institutions representing the wider society. Analysis could include: the irony of Leah confiding in Phil despite his silence; Leah's antagonistic description of Phil suggesting his lack of interest in anyone or anything else; Richard's inability to understand others in the universe being a metaphor for people within a community knowing that there are others out there but being unable to empathise or form connections with one another.

Pages 50–51

Quick Test

1. He sees it as asking moral questions of the audience, including whether murder is ever justified.
2. Characters like Leah, who challenge Phil, or those who are less directly involved in Adam's death.
3. Phil (immoral) although he might see himself otherwise; Cathy (amoral), who is motivated by personal success and enjoyment.
4. All the characters behave immorally, by covering up Adam's death. Arguably Adam is the only moral character.

Exam Practice

Answers could include consideration of which characters are moral or focus on the question of one character's morality. Analysis could explore Danny's use of common idiom suggesting that accusations of immorality are a taint, or the pauses showing Leah's disbelief at Cathy and Cathy's hesitation in admitting her immoral act.

Pages 52–53

Quick Test

1. Personal responsibility and collective responsibility.
2. It is unclear – probably not Leah and Phil but possibly all of the others.
3. All of them, as they participate in the cover-up of his death, tolerating his bullying and torture.
4. Phil and Cathy. Leah could be considered as having some collective responsibility as she seems to understand what is happening and protests, but she isn't directly involved in planning or carrying out the murder.
5. John Tate and Danny as they leave the group before Adam returns. Brian's breakdown leaves him unable to make rational decisions so he too is not responsible.

Exam Practice

Answers could include the different types of responsibility people hold. Analysis could explore: Leah's assumption of collective responsibility (before she hears of Adam's death); Leah's accusatory language towards Phil and her sarcastic use of idiom showing her upset; Phil's repeated use of 'this' and short utterances creating a sense of logical progression, which removes responsibility as it suggests the events were out of their control.

Pages 54–55

Quick Test

1. A strong leader, and followers in a clear hierarchy.
2. Collective pronouns 'we'/'us' contrasting with 'everyone else'.
3. Leah, until the end. Lou is loyal to Cathy in the final act. Richard is most loyal to Phil.
4. John Tate and Danny leave the gang completely. Phil could be loyal – his plans seem designed to help the others – but he has separated from them at the end, having not performed any of the actions himself but manipulated others into doing so.

Answers

Exam Practice

Analysis could include: the chimp metaphor representing Adam/Brian and the others as the gang on the other side; Lou's hesitation/repetition suggesting her desire to follow Cathy, which foreshadows her future role as Cathy's best friend; John's language of 'sides' to rule using division and to create an impression of the gang as protective of its own.

Pages 56–57
Quick Test

1. In conflicting ways, for example, describing people's need to seem happy. She is desperate to assure Phil's happiness.
2. Recognising it is an appearance or pretence, about what people expect happy to look like.
3. They come together as a community with a sense of purpose in mourning Adam.
4. Phil connects happiness with insanity after Adam's return, suggesting they share similar characteristics.
5. Some aren't happy, separated from one another (John Tate, Danny) or suffering from anxiety (Brian). Some offstage characters might be happy, but it's ambiguous as we don't see them.

Exam Practice

Answers could explore Kelly's use of Leah to explore happiness and the moment when this occurs, at the opening of 2.2 when Adam is believed to be dead. Answers could consider happiness as a performance emphasised by the language of pretence/seeing. Analysis could contrast the negative language of 'grief' and 'mad', seeing the happiness of some people as more important than the happiness of all.

Pages 62–63
Quick Test

1. Understanding of the whole text, specific analysis and terminology, awareness of the relevance of context, a well-structured essay and accurate writing.
2. Planning focuses your thoughts and allows you to produce a well-structured essay.
3. Quotations give you more opportunities to enable you to do specific AO2 analysis.

Exam Practice

Answers might include: Phil's personal responsibility in planning the cover-up and direct instructions to others; the development in his character when he instructs deliberate murder; his insistence he is acting for the good of everybody. Analysis could look at his methods of control, for example, silences with Leah, or his developing use of violence, (threatening Brian (2.3) and then putting a bag on his head (3.3)) or Kelly's use of food to portray Phil's seeming indifference to the rest of the group.

Pages 68–69
Quick Test

1. Understanding of the whole text, specific analysis and terminology, awareness of the relevance of context, a well-structured essay and accurate writing.
2. Planning focuses your thoughts and allows you to produce a well-structured essay.
3. Quotations give you more opportunities to enable you to do specific AO2 analysis.

Exam Practice

Answers could explore different ideas of what community is, for example, the gang versus the rest of society, and the alienation that the group feel after behaving in a way outside social norms. Analysis could include: Leah's monologues on the performance of happiness, suggesting that there isn't honesty in society; regular inclusive language (everyone, we, together), which serves to keep the gang together and also distinct from the rest of society; the fragmentation of the gang by the end, either disappearing offstage or into small groups.

Pages 66–67 and 72–73

Use the mark scheme below to self-assess your strengths and weaknesses. Work up from the bottom, putting a tick by things you have fully accomplished, a ½ by skills that are in place but need securing and underlining areas that need development. The estimated grade boundaries are included so you can assess your progress towards your target grade.

Grade	AO1 (12 marks)	AO2 (12 marks)	AO3 (6 marks)	AO4 (4 marks)
6–7+	A convincing, well-structured essay that answers the question fully. Quotations and references are well chosen and integrated into sentences. The response covers the whole play.	Analysis of the full range of Kelly's methods. Thorough exploration of the effects of these methods. Accurate range of subject terminology.	Exploration is linked to specific aspects of the play's contexts to show a detailed understanding.	Consistent high level of accuracy. Vocabulary and sentences are used to make ideas clear and precise.
4–5	A clear essay that always focuses on the exam question. Quotations and references support ideas effectively. The response refers to different points in the play.	Explanation of Kelly's different methods. Clear understanding of the effects of these methods. Accurate use of subject terminology.	References to relevant aspects of context show a clear understanding.	Good level of accuracy. Vocabulary and sentences help to make ideas clear.
2–3	The essay has some good ideas that are mostly relevant. Some quotations and references are used to support the ideas.	Identification of some different methods used by Kelly to convey meaning. Some subject terminology.	Some awareness of how ideas in the play link to its context.	Reasonable level of accuracy. Errors do not get in the way of the essay making sense.